KU-661-202

LIMITATION OF LIABILITY

Merchant Shipping Act, 1894
(Section 503 and subsequent amendments)

WITHDRAWN

i

Published and distributed by
FAIRPLAY PUBLICATIONS LTD.
52/54 Southwark Street, London SE1 1UJ
Telephone: 01-403 3164
Telex: 884595 FPLAY G

ISBN 0 905045 63 7

Copyright © 1985 by Fairplay Publications Ltd.

Front cover: "Marion" — a question of 'actual fault or privity'.
(Photo by R. Kleyn)

All rights reserved. No part of this publication may be reproduced or transmitted, in any form or by any means, electronic, mechanical, photocopying, recording, or any information storage or retrieval system without permission in writing from the publisher.

Typeset by JJ Typographics, Rochford, Essex.
Printed by Mayhew McCrimmon Printers Ltd., Gt Wakering, Essex.

To all my friends in the shipping and marine insurance
world for their continued support and assistance.

Acknowledgements

THE author wishes to express his thanks to Phyllis Gorton for her very necessary encouragement and support in the production of this and previous books, and above all for her invaluable expertise in the checking of the drafts, texts and proofs.

The author is especially indebted also to Chris Hewer who has burned up a great deal of midnight oil as reader of these works in order to present them in a proper readable form.

About the Author

The author will be widely known in the world of marine insurance and shipping for his work in relation to the adjustment of claims, as between shipowners and carriers of goods by sea and marine insurers, arising out of the question of liability in respect of cargo loss and damage occurring during the course of the carriage of goods by sea.

He was for many years the examiner to the Chartered Insurance Institute on this subject and is presently a marine consultant in this and other fields relating to cargo loss and damage. He is a past member of the Royal Institute of Navigation and Institute of Transport.

His previous titles in Fairplay's legal series include "Shipping and the Law", "Hague Rules Law Digest", "The Hamburg Rules", "Bills of Lading Law", "International Cargo Carriers' Liabilities", "Legal Developments in Maritime Commerce", "The Right of Appeal", and "Time Charter Withdrawals".

LIMITATION OF LIABILITY

CONTENTS

Certain recurring problems arising out of contested applications for a decree of limitation of liability under the provisions of Section 503 of the Merchant Shipping Act, 1894, as amended by subsequent Acts, are made the subject of individual chapters in which, amongst other things, the leading cases on such problems are grouped together and discussed under one head. The following is a list, in alphabetical order, of the articles concerned in this section, followed by a reference to the problem discussed.

CHAPTER I **Actual fault or privity** 1
The intention, interpretation and effect of the words contained in sections 502 and 503 of the Merchant Shipping Act, 1894, and amending Acts.

CHAPTER II **Alter Ego** 7
The person who may be found to don the mantle of the shipowner.

CHAPTER III **Collisions between ships** 15
(See also pilotage)
Some guidelines as to circumstances in which shipowners may or may not succeed in proving absence of their actual fault or privity.

CHAPTER IV **Damage to property ashore** 27
The nature of the burden upon shipowners to prove absence of fault or privity.

CHAPTER V **Distinct and separate occasions** 33
Where one damage succeeds another can the second damage be claimed as negligence arising out of the first?

CHAPTER VI **Dock owners and wharf owners** 37
Their rights to limitation of liability under the provisions of the Merchant Shipping Acts.

CHAPTER VII **Management of ship** 41
The responsibilities of the shipowner *vis-a-vis* the provisions of the Merchant Shipping Acts with regard to limitation of liability.

CHAPTER VIII   **Master and/or other officers part owners of**   53
                     colliding vessel
                     Interpretation of section 503 of Merchant Shipping
                     Act in regard thereto.

CHAPTER IX   **Pilotage**   57
                     Collisions arising out of fault or neglect in pilotage-
                     — Some facets of the problem of limitation in
                     relation thereto.

CHAPTER X   **Security or bail provided by arrest of vessel**   63
                     The effect of the Merchant Shipping Act's limitation
                     of liability in regard thereto.

CHAPTER XI   **Ships within meaning of the Merchant Shipping Acts**   65
                     Whether dumb barges in tow were ships within the
                     meaning of the Acts.

CHAPTER XII   **Supervision of Navigation**   67
                     (See also Supply of Charts, navigational and
                     operational information)
                     Responsibilities of the shipowner *vis-a-vis* the
                     provisions of the Merchant Shipping Acts with regard
                     to limitation of liability.

CHAPTER XIII   **Supply of charts, navigational and operational**   75
                     information
                     Effect of shipowners' failure to ensure vessels
                     navigated with up to date information upon right to
                     limit liability under the provisions of the Merchant
                     Shipping Acts.

CHAPTER XIV   **Towage contracts**   83
                     In relation to Section 503 of the Merchant Shipping
                     Act, 1894.

CHAPTER XV   **Tug and Tow**   85
                     Limitation of liability — when tug and tow in same
                     ownership — when tug and tow in different
                     ownership — basis of limitation *vis-a-vis* tonnage of
                     tug and tow — position when grounded vessel taken
                     in tow by sister ship — etc.

CHAPTER XVI   **Unseaworthiness**   91
                     The conception of seaworthiness within the meaning
                     of the Merchant Shipping Act and illustrations of the
                     effect of Section 503 of the Act and amending Acts
                     in relation to limitation of liability to property
                     damage caused by unseaworthiness.

CHAPTER XVII   **Wreck raising expenses**   97
Whether expenses constitute loss or damage —
whether within coverage of limitation of liability in
the Merchant Shipping Acts.

CHAPTER XVIII   **Other matters of special interest**   101
1 — Limitation of time for bringing claims against the
limitation fund
2 — Limitation when only one claim arises
3 — Meaning of person being carried in ship
4 — Position as regards limitation when cargo owned by
crown
5 — Salvage services
6 — When barges operate without motive power

PREFACE

FOR those concerned with the day-to-day business of seaborne commerce, with particular reference to the adjustment of claims arising out of damage to cargo carried or to other property, ashore or afloat, by the vessel concerned, it is most useful to be able to reach to the shelf for a compendium from which may be sought the necessary guidelines for the solution of problems when dispute arises.

It is to this end that the author has directed his efforts to the problems that have arisen out of the interpretation of the provisions of Section 503 of the Merchant Shipping Act, 1894, and amending Acts, concerning the right of the shipowner, wharf owner or others to limit their liability arising out of the negligence of their agents or servants.

When shipowners or others have to accept liability for damage done to cargo or other property ashore or afloat, if they are of the opinion that they can lessen the amount of their liability by invoking the provisions of Section 503 of the Merchant Shipping Act, 1894 and amending Acts, then naturally they will offer the claimant payment based upon the tonnage limitation provided for in the amending Acts. However, it may well be that the claimant will contest the right of the shipowner or other party seeking to limit liability, upon the ground that the right to limit liability under the Acts has been extinguished because the damage done to the property of the claimant has not arisen without the actual fault or privity of the party seeking to limit liability.

It is at this point that both parties to the dispute may wish to lay their hands on the guidelines of the Courts laid down from time to time, with the immediate possibility of placing their finger on an identical case which has been before the Court, or a case which may have a direct bearing upon the issue involved, and so enable some amicable settlement of the dispute to be reached. The author hopes that this book will have achieved that purpose.

The book is divided into eighteen chapters, so captioned as to provide an immediate reference in order to identify the nature of the problem with which the parties in a dispute may be involved. Then, in each of the chapters, there will be found contained a further breakdown showing the individual disputes dealt with, among which may be found an almost identical case with which the parties are concerned, or a case which may have, if not a direct bearing upon the issue between them, an indirect bearing, which in any event should provide the necessary guidelines for the resolution of their dispute.

Additionally an index has been included to provide an immediate reference to the individual problems contained within the chapters, together with the chapter reference and the name of the law case concerned, under the short title of the name of the vessel concerned, by means of which the reader will be able to pin-point any case relative to a particular problem.

INTRODUCTION

MOST, if not all, major maritime nations have statutory provisions providing in some form or other the right of a shipowner to limit his liability in certain circumstances when loss or damage has been caused to the property of others by his vessel. Such form of legislation has been in existence in some Continental nations for over two centuries and its importance is recognised internationally. There have indeed been a number of international conventions in this present century dealing with the subject of limitation of shipowners' liability and how it is to be regulated.

The purpose of such legislation in the United Kingdom, and no doubt in other countries, is to provide some relief and protection to shipowners in respect of loss or damage caused to other property by their vessel when such loss or damage has been caused without their actual fault or privity. In the United Kingdom such relief is provided by the Merchant Shipping Act, 1894, as amended by subsequent acts. In its present amended form, it provides the shipowner with the right to limit liability by Section 503 of the Merchant Shipping Act, 1894, as amended by the Merchant Shipping (Liability of Shipowners and Others) Act, 1958. Its relevant statutory provisions provide that "the owners of a ship, British or foreign, shall not where all or any of the following occurrences take place without their actual fault or privity (that is to say) (d) where any loss or damage is caused to any property ... or any rights are infringed through the act or omission of any person (whether on board the ship or not) in the navigation or management of the ship ... or through any other act or omission of any person on board the ship, be liable in damages beyond the following amounts." These amounts, which are based upon the tonnage of the ship, are regulated from time to time by international conventions and are given effect in the United Kingdom by amendments to the Act of 1894.

In order to be successful in a limitation action, the shipowner has the burden of proving that such loss or damage caused by his vessel was not the result of, and was not contributed to by, any fault or privity of his own. It was laid down many years ago that the words "actual fault or privity" infer something personal to the shipowner, something blameworthy in him, as distinguished from constructive fault or privity such as the fault or privity of his servants or agents. But the words "actual fault" are not confined to affirmative or positive acts by way of fault, and if a shipowner be guilty of an act or omission to do something which he ought to have done, he is no less guilty of an actual fault than if the act had been one of commission.

To avail himself of the statutory defence, he must show that he himself is not blameworthy for having either done or omitted to do something or been privy to something. It is not necessary to show knowledge and if he has means of knowledge which he ought to have used and does not avail himself of, his omission so to do may be fault, and, if so, it is an actual fault and he may be refused a decree of limitation of liability.

But there are other equally important facets of the problem, not least of which is the problem which faces a limited company since the "owners", within the meaning of this particular section of the Act, must be the person or persons with whom the chief management of the company's business resides, and the company's active and directing will must consequently be sought in the person of somebody who for some purposes may be called an agent, but who is really the directing mind and will of the corporation, the very ego and centre of the personality of the corporation; in other words the alter ego, somebody who is not a servant or agent for whom the company is liable, but somebody for whom the company is liable because his action is the very action of the company itself.

This poses a problem for the shipowner in the case of an action for the limitation of liability, the nature of which is outlined in this book in the chapter headed "Alter Ego". It is not enough that the negligence or fault, leading to the damage to other property, should be the fault of a servant or agent of the company in order to enable the shipowner to be successful in an action for limitation of liability; the fault must also be one which is not the fault of the owner or a fault to which the owner is privy.

Mention should also be made of the position of the shipowner, in the case of a limited company, when he delegates the management of his ship to another limited company. It seems clear that in such circumstances, in the event that the owners of the vessel causing damage to other property seek a decree of limitation, the Court will look to the managing company when considering whether the owners of the vessel are guilty of actual fault, and it will be the practice to determine who should be regarded as the alter ego of that company.

One of the prime considerations leading to the enforcement of Section 503 of the Merchant Shipping Act, 1894, was no doubt the liability of the shipowner in respect of damage by collision at sea, bearing in mind the great potential liability of the blameworthy vessel in the event that the other vessel became a total loss together with her cargo, and, of course, the great potential liability arising out of death and injury. The coverage of the Act of 1894 has been extended from time to time.

The Merchant Shipping Act 1900, among other things, extended the Act of 1894 to cover any loss or damage caused to property or rights of any kind "whether on land or on water".

The Merchant Shipping Act, 1921, amongst other things, extends the right of limitation to the hirer of any barge who has contracted to take over the sole charge and management thereof and is responsible for the navigation, manning and equipment thereof.

The provisions of the Act also apply to barge navigation and towage. All of this has provided a fund of knowledge as to the manner in which the provisions of the Merchant Shipping Acts should be interpreted in relation to the many disputes arising out of limitation of liability, involving questions of navigation and management and other ancillary problems, which will be found outlined in this book.

The actual limits of liability based upon the vessel's tonnage have not been included for the reason that the amounts to which a shipowner may be entitled to limit liability are amended from time to time, as witness the amendments in this respect should the 1976 Convention be ratified and the Merchant Shipping Act, 1979, come into force.

THE OUTLOOK FOR THE FUTURE

Introducing the 1976 Convention on Limitation of Liability and Schedule 4 of the Merchant Shipping Act, 1979.

THE Merchant Shipping Act, 1894, contains a multitude of provisions covering a great variety of subjects, ranging from qualification for owning British ships, registration procedures, certificates of competency for masters and seamen, safety, liability of shipowners, wreck and salvage etc., covering some fourteen parts and over seven hundred sections, as amended, from time to time by amending Acts. This present volume has reference to the interpretation and effect of that section of the Act relative to the limitation of the liability of the shipowner in respect of damage to other property done by his vessel either shore or afloat, namely Section 503 and amending Acts relative thereto.

In reaching this appreciation of the right of a shipowner to limit his liability and the circumstances in which a plea for limitation of liability, under the provisions of Section 503, may be granted or refused, there have been examined a large number of selected disputes which have come before the Courts over the years terminating with the case of the *Marion* decided in the House of Lords in April, 1984. The law, as presently laid down by these cases before the Courts, provides the necessary guidance for commercial interests in assessing their relative positions when dispute should arise as to the right of a shipowner to limit liability under Section 503 of the Merchant Shipping Act, 1894, and amending Acts.

However, in the event that the required number of States ratify the Convention on Limitation of Liability for Maritime Claims 1976, some twelve months later Schedule 4 of the Merchant Shipping Act 1979 will be brought into effect which, among many other matters, will have some effect on the present law relative to the provisions of Section 503 of the Merchant Shipping Act, 1894, and amending Acts, for the reason that certain provisions of the Convention are set out in the Merchant Shipping Act, 1979, (Schedule 4) which will come into force twelve months after the required number of States have ratified the Convention.

When that date is reached there will need to be considered, *inter alia* (and so far as this book is concerned) the effect of Article 4 of Schedule 4 in the Merchant Shipping Act, 1979, which provides that "A person shall not be entitled to limit his liability if it is proved that the loss resulted from his personal act or omission, committed with the intent to cause such loss, or recklessly and with knowledge that such loss would probably result."

Presently, Section 503 provides for the limitation of the liability of the shipowner, British or foreign, where loss or damage is caused "without their actual fault or privity". The word "personal" would seem to imply a more restrictive approach as to the persons embraced in the words "owners of a ship" and so make it much more difficult to contest an owner's plea for limitation. To be borne in mind also is the definition of the term "shipowner" in Article 1 paragraph 2 of Schedule 4 of the Merchant Shipping Act, 1979, qualified in Part II to mean "any" ship not "seagoing ship". However, in considering the problems in the test cases which will no doubt be brought in the years to come, the Courts will lean heavily upon the law as it presently exists, particularly that laid down in the case of the *Lady Gwendolen* in the Court of Appeal and the ruling delivered in the House of Lords in the case of the *Marion.*

Schedule 4 of the Merchant Shipping Act, 1979, Article 1 (persons entitled to limit liability), Article 2 (Claims subject to limitation), Article 3 (Claims excepted from limitation), Article 4 (conduct barring limitation) and Article 5 (counter-claims) are set out below as coming within the ambit of this book, from which it will be seen, amongst other things, that the Act, unlike the Act of 1894 and amending Acts, makes special provisions for the right of limitation to those rendering salvage services in respect of consequential loss therefrom but excludes claims for salvage or contribution in general average. Also, particularly relevant to this book is the provision in respect of claims for wreck raising or removal.

SCHEDULE 4

CONVENTION ON LIMITATION OF LIABILITY FOR MARITIME CLAIMS 1976

PART I

TEXT OF CONVENTION

CHAPTER I. THE RIGHT OF LIMITATION

ARTICLE I

Persons entitled to limit liability

1. Shipowners and salvors, as hereinafter defined, may limit their liability in accordance with the rules of this Convention for claims set out in Article 2.

2. The term "shipowner" shall mean the owner, charterer, manager or operator of a seagoing ship.

3. Salvor shall mean any person rendering services in direct connexion with salvage operations. Salvage operations shall also include operations referred to in Article 2, paragraph 1 (*d*), (*e*) and (*f*).

4. If any claims set out in Article 2 are made against any person for whose act, neglect or default the shipowner or salvor is responsible, such person shall be entitled to avail himself of the limitation of liability provided for in this Convention.

5. In this Convention the liability of a shipowner shall include liability in an action brought against the vessel herself.

6. An insurer of liability for claims subject to limitation in accordance with the rules of this Convention shall be entitled to the benefits of this Convention to the same extent as the assured himself.

7. The act of invoking limitation of liability shall not constitute an admission of liability.

ARTICLE 2

Claims subject to limitation

1. Subject to Articles 3 and 4 the following claims, whatever the basis of liability may be, shall be subject to limitation of liability:
   (a) claims in respect of loss of life or personal injury or loss of or damage to property (including damage to harbour works, basins and waterways and aids to navigation), occurring on board or in direct connexion with the operation of the ship or with salvage operations, and consequential loss resulting therefrom;
   (b) claims in respect of loss resulting from delay in the carriage by sea of cargo, passengers or their luggage;
   (c) claims in respect of other loss resulting from infringement of rights other than contractual rights, occurring in direct connexion with the operation of the ship or salvage operations;
   (d) claims in respect of the raising, removal, destruction or the rendering harmless of a ship which is sunk, wrecked, stranded or abandoned, including anything that is or has been on board such ship;
   (e) claims in respect of the removal, destruction or the rendering harmless of the cargo of the ship;
   (f) claims of a person other than the person liable in respect of measures taken in order to avert or minimize loss for which the person liable may limit his liability in accordance with this Convention, and further loss caused by such measures.

2. Claims set out in paragraph 1 shall be subject to limitation of liability even if brought by way of recourse or for indemnity under a contract or otherwise. However, claims set out under paragraph 1(d), (e) and (f) shall not be subject to limitation of liability to the extent that they relate to remuneration under a contract with the person liable.

ARTICLE 3

Claims excepted from limitation

The rules of this Convention shall not apply to:
   (a) claims for salvage or contribution in general average;
   (b) claims for oil pollution damage within the meaning of the International Convention on Civil Liability for Oil Pollution Damage dated 29th

November 1969 or of any amendment or Protocol thereto which is in force;

(c) claims subject to any international convention or national legislation governing or prohibiting limitation of liability for nuclear damage;

(d) claims against the shipowner of a nuclear ship for nuclear damage;

(e) claims by servants of the shipowner or salvor whose duties are connected with the ship or the salvage operations, including claims of their heirs, dependents or other persons entitled to make such claims, if under the law governing the contract of service between the shipowner or salvor and such servants the shipowner or salvor is not entitled to limit his liability in respect of such claims, or if he is by such law only permitted to limit his liability to an amount greater than that provided for in Article 6.

ARTICLE 4

Conduct barring limitation

A person liable shall not be entitled to limit his liability if it is proved that the loss resulted from his personal act or omission, committed with the intent to cause such loss, or recklessly and with knowledge that such loss would probably result.

ARTICLE 5

Counterclaims

Where a person entitled to limitation of liability under the rules of this Convention has a claim against the claimant arising out of the same occurrence, their respective claims shall be set off against each other and the provisions of this Convention shall only apply to the balance, if any.

Although in the future, when Schedule 4 of the Merchant Shipping Act, 1979, giving effect to the Convention on Limitation of Liability for Maritime Claims 1976, comes into force, litigation will later follow in order to test the meaning and effect of certain new provisions introduced into the Act thereby, the existing law cases establishing the legal precedents to be observed in the determination of the right of the shipowner and others to limit their liability in certain circumstances under the provisions of the Merchant Shipping Act, 1894, will remain firmly entrenched. *(See also, "The Outlook for the Future".)*

The sections of the Merchant Shipping Acts relevant to this volume

THE MERCHANT SHIPPING ACT, 1894
SECTION 503 (1)

The owners of a ship, British or foreign, shall not where all or any of the following occurrences take place without their actual fault or privity; (that is to say)

(*a*) Where any loss of life or personal injury is caused to any person being carried in a ship;

(*b*) Where any damage or loss is caused to any goods, merchandise, or other things whatsoever on board the ship;

(*c*) Where any loss of life or personal injury is caused to any person carried in any other vessel by reason of the improper navigation of the ship;

(*d*) Where any loss or damage is caused to any other vessel, or to any goods, merchandise, or other things whatsoever on board any other vessel, by reason of the improper navigation of the ship;

be liable to pay damages beyond the following amounts; (that is to say)

(The amounts are then listed but are subject to amendment from time to time by amending Acts)

Sub-Section (2)

Sets out the basis upon which the tonnage of a vessel shall be calculated for the purposes of limitation of liability.

Sub-Section (3)

The owner of every sea-going ship or share therein shall be liable in respect of every such loss of life, personal injury, loss of or damage to vessels, goods, merchandise, or things as aforesaid arising on distinct occasions to the same extent as if no other loss, injury or damage had arisen.

THE MERCHANT SHIPPING (LIABILITY OF SHIPOWNERS AND OTHERS) ACT, 1900

Section (1)

The limitation of the liability of the owners of any ship set by Section 503 of the Merchant Shipping Act, 1894, in respect of loss of or damage to vessels, goods, merchandise or other things, shall extend and apply to all cases where (without their actual fault or privity) any loss or damage is caused to property or rights of any kind, whether on land or on water, or whether fixed or moveable, by reason of the improper navigation or management of the ship.

Section (2)

(1) The owners of any dock or canal, or a harbour authority or a conservancy authority, as defined by the Merchant Shipping Act, 1894, shall not, where without their actual fault or privity any loss or damage is caused to any vessel or vessels, or to any goods, merchandise or other things whatsoever on board any vessel or vessels, be liable to damages beyond an aggregate amount not exceeding ... for each ton of the tonnage of the largest registered British ship which, at the time of such loss or damage occurring, is, or within the period of five years previous thereto has been, within the area over which such dock or canal owner, harbour authority, or conservancy authority, performs any duty or exercises any power. A ship shall not be deemed to have been within the area over which a harbour authority or a conservancy authority performs any duty, or exercises any powers, by reason only that it has been built or fitted out within such area, or that it has taken shelter within or passed through such area on a voyage between two places both situated outside that area, or that it has been loaded or unloaded mails or passengers within that area ...

(4) for the purposes of this section the term "dock" shall include wet docks and basins, tidal docks and basins, locks, cuts, entrances, dry docks, graving docks, grid-irons, slips, quays, wharves, piers, stages, landing places and jetties.

(5) For the purposes of this section the term "owners of dock or canal" shall include any person or authority having the control and management of any dock or canal, as the case may be.

Section (3)

The limitation of liability under this Act shall relate to the whole of any losses and damages which may arise upon any one distinct occasion, although such losses and damages may be sustained by more than one person, and shall apply whether the liability arises at common law or under any general or private Act of Parliament, and notwithstanding anything contained in such Act.

THE MERCHANT SHIPPING (LIABILITY OF SHIPOWNERS AND OTHERS) ACT, 1958.

This Act amends the provisions of Section 503 of the Merchant Shipping Act, 1894, and the following are the amendments, so far as concerns this present volume, to the Act of 1894.

Section (1)

The owners of a ship, British or foreign, shall not, where all or any of the following occurrences take place without their actual fault or privity (that is to say)

    (a) Where any loss of life or personal injury is caused to any person being carried in the ship;

    (b) Where any damage or loss is caused to any goods, merchandise, or other things whatsoever on board the ship;

(c) Where any loss of life or personal injury is caused to any person not carried in the ship through the act or omission of any person (whether on board the ship or not) in the navigation or management of the ship or in the loading, carriage or discharge of its cargo or in the embarkation of its passengers, or through any other act or omission of any person on board the ship.

(d) Where any loss or damage is caused to any property (other than any property mentioned in paragraph (b) of this sub-section) or any rights are infringed through the act or omission of any person (whether on board the ship or not) in the navigation or management of the ship, or in the loading, carriage or discharge of its cargo or in the embarkation, carriage or disembarkation of its passengers, or through any other act or omission of any person on board the ship;

be liable to damages beyond the following amounts ...
(there are then specified the amounts).

Section (1) sub-section (3) of the 1958 Act reads

The (Secretary of State for Trade) may from time to time by order made by statutory instrument specify the amounts which for the purpose of this section are to be taken as equivalent to three thousand one hundred and one thousand gold francs respectively.

Sub-section (4) provides that

Where money has been paid into Court (or in Scotland, consigned in Court) in respect of any liability to which a limit is set as aforesaid, the ascertainment of that limit shall not be affected by a subsequent variation of the amounts specified under sub-section (3) of this section unless the amount paid or consigned was less than the limit as ascertained in accordance with the order then in force under that sub-section.

Section (3) of the Act of 1958 reads:

(1) The persons whose liability in connection with a ship is excluded or limited by part VIII of the Merchant Shipping Act, 1894, shall include any charterer and any person interested in or in possession of the ship, and, in particular, any manager or operator of the ship.

(2) In relation to a claim arising from the act or omission of any person in his capacity as master or member of the crew or (otherwise in that capacity) in the course of his employment as a servant of the owners or of any such person as is mentioned in sub-section (1) of this section:

(a) the persons whose liability is excluded or limited as aforesaid shall also include the master, member of the crew or servant, and, in a case where the master or member of the crew is the servant of a person whose liability would not be excluded or limited apart from this paragraph, the person whose servant he is; and

(b) the liability of the master, member of the crew or servant himself shall be excluded or limited as aforesaid notwithstanding his actual fault or privity in that capacity, except in the cases mentioned in

paragraph (*ii*) of section five hundred and two of the said Act of
1894.

THE MERCHANT SHIPPING ACT, 1921
Section 1 (2)

... extends the right of limitation to the hirer of any barge who has
contracted to take over the sole charge and management thereof and is
responsible for the navigation, manning and equipment thereof.

CHAPTER I

Actual fault or privity

The intention, interpretation and effect of the words contained in Sections 502 and 503 of the Merchant Shipping Act, 1894, and amending Acts.

THE right of a shipowner to limit his liability in certain circumstances is a statutory right of long standing and most, if not all, maritime nations have statutory provisions to that effect. So far as the United Kingdom is concerned, that right is laid down in Section 503 of the Merchant Shipping Act, 1894, and in subsequent amendments to that Act. Section 502 goes further than the limitation of liability and gives the shipowner complete immunity from liability in respect of loss or damage caused to goods by reason of fire on board the vessel, and, in certain circumstances, the loss of precious metals, jewelry and the like. But, with the exception of the case of the *Edward Dawson (Lloyd's Law Reports March 8, 1915),* on which the issue of actual fault or privity generally hinges, this book is concerned with Section 503 of the Act of 1894, as amended by subsequent Acts, limiting the liability of the shipowner in respect of loss or damage to goods or merchandise.

Unquestionably, the intention of this statutory right to limitation of liability is to relieve shipowners of the consequences of negligent acts of their servants in the navigation or the management of the ship, and it no doubt stems from the fact that in the ordinary course of events the owner of a vessel, or a member of the boardroom of a company, is not present on board the ship in the day-to-day navigation or running of the ship, the general duties of which must, generally speaking, be in the hands of subordinates. But, as this book will show, the owners of a vessel or, in the case of a company, the boardroom cannot divest themselves of all responsibilities in this respect, because the Merchant Shipping Act, 1894, provides that the owners of a vessel can limit liability only subject to such loss or damage having occurred without their actual fault or privity, to which must now be added, because of the rulings of the Courts in cases where an action for a decree of limitation of liability is contested by the claimants, a burden on the owners of the vessel to prove also that such loss or damage as has been done by their vessel has not been contributed to by the actual fault or privity of the owners of the vessel.

In cases where a limited company is concerned, it is the practice to determine who should be regarded as the "alter ego" of the company (see the relevant chapter in this book under that caption) and where a vessel is owned by one limited company and managed by another limited company the Court will look to the managing company when considering whether the owners are guilty of actual fault, so that in such circumstances it will be the alter ego of the managing company which will need to be determined.

The words "actual fault or privity" infer something personal to the owner, something blameworthy in him, as distinguished from constructive fault or privity such as the fault or privity of his servants or agents. But the words "actual fault" are not confined to affirmative or positive acts by way of fault, and if the owner of a vessel is guilty of an act of omission to do something which he ought to have done, he is no less guilty of an actual fault than if the act had been one of commission. In order to avail himself of the statutory defence, he must show that he himself is not blameworthy for having either done or omitted to do something or has been privy to something. If is not necessary to show knowledge and if he has the means of knowledge which he ought to have used and does not avail himself of such, his omission so to do may be a fault, and, if so, it is an actual fault and the owner of the vessel cannot claim the benefit of Section 503 of the Merchant Shipping Act, 1894, as amended by subsequent Acts.

The cornerstone of this piece of legal interpretation is to be found in a dispute which came before the House of Lords in 1915, the case of the *Edward Dawson,* otherwise known by its full title *Lennard's Carrying Company Ltd. v. Asiatic Petroleum Company Ltd.*

The case of the *Edward Dawson* did not, however, arise out of action for the limitation of liability but out of an action in which the owners sought to avoid liability under the provisions of Section 502 of the Merchant Shipping Act, 1894, which provides that the owner of a British seagoing ship, or any share therein, shall not be liable to make good to any extent whatever any loss or damage happening without his actual fault or privity where any goods, merchandise, or other things whatsoever taken in or put on board his ship are lost or damaged by reason of fire on board the ship.

The *Edward Dawson* had loaded a cargo of benzine at Novorossisk, Russia, for carriage to Rotterdam. During the course of her voyage she ran into heavy weather and, because of the defective condition of her boilers, she could not muster sufficient steam power to face the gale and was driven ashore. The stranding of the vessel damaged her tanks to such an extent that some of the benzine escaped and came into contact with the combustion chambers of the boilers which caused an explosion resulting in the loss of the ship and her cargo of benzine. The question that now arose was whether what happened took place without the actual fault or privity of the owners of the ship.

The owners of the ship were a limited company and the ship was managed by another limited company, namely John M. Lennard & Sons. Mr. J.M. Lennard was the active director of the company, and was also a director of Lennard's Carrying Company Ltd., who were claiming the protection of the Act. The Court found that Mr. J.M. Lennard was unable to prove that he did not know or could excuse himself for not having known of the defective condition of the boilers, which amounted to unseaworthiness. The Court also found that Mr. Lennard was the person who was registered in the ship's register and was designated as the person to whom the management of the vessel was entrusted.

The Court said that it must be upon the true construction of Section 502 of

2

the Act that the fault or privity is the fault or privity of somebody who is not merely a servant or agent for whom the company is liable but somebody for whom the company is liable because his action is the very action of the company itself. It is not enough that the fault should be the fault of a servant in order to exonerate the owner of the vessel; the fault must also be one which is not the fault of the owner, or a fault to which the owner is privy.

Mr. Lennard did not go into Court to rebut the presumption of liability and the Court had no satisfactory evidence as to what the constitution of the company was or what Mr. Lennard's position was, and the only evidence was that of the secretary who told the Court that he was secretary not only to the company but also to the managing company and the Court found that the inference to be drawn was that the officials of the two companies were very much the same and transacted very much the same business. In these circumstances it was held that the company and Mr. Lennard had not discharged the burden of proof which was upon them, and that it had to be taken that the unseaworthiness existing at the commencement of the voyage from Novorossisk, was an unseaworthiness which did not exist without the actual fault or privity of the owning company.

The ruling of the House of Lords in that case provided the guidelines which need to be observed whenever questions arise over the nature of the protection afforded the owners of a vessel by Sections 502 and 503 of the Merchant Shipping Act, 1894, or the subsequent amendments thereto. Those guidelines have now been built upon by the Courts in considering whether or not a shipowner is entitled to a decree of limitation of liability under the provisions of Section 503, in respect of loss or damage caused by his vessel to property afloat or ashore.

For the purposes of this chapter, two cases have been selected, out of the many which have come before the Courts, in which an action for the limitation of liability has been contested on the grounds that the casualty did not occur without the actual fault or privity of the owners of the vessel. Reference is first made to the case of the *Lady Gwendolen (Lloyd's Law Reports — 1964 — 2 — 99 and Court of Appeal — 1965 — 1 — 335)* when the owners of that vessel sought a decree of limitation of liability in respect of the damage done by their vessel when she collided with and sank the motor vessel *Freshfield* which was anchored in the River Mersey.

The *Lady Gwendolen* was, at the time of the collision, proceeding at full speed in conditions of dense fog, and although the owners of the vessel admitted their liability they claimed from the Court a declaration limiting their liability. This was contested on the ground that the collision did not occur without the owners' actual fault or privity, on the grounds (1)(a) that they failed to instruct the master of the vessel to place considerations of safety above those of keeping schedule, or to see that such instructions were observed, and (b) failed to instruct the master not to proceed at excessive speed in fog or to see that the master complied with that instruction; and (2)(a) failed to ensure that the master or mate were properly instructed in the use of radar, including the fact that radar did not entitle them to proceed at full speed in fog; and (b) failed to instruct the master as to the necessity of a mate being on the bridge when using radar.

Evidence was given before the Court that the master of this vessel habitually proceeded at excessive speed in fog and that at the time of the collision the master was on the bridge, alone with the helmsman, proceeding at full speed. In the trial Court it was held that the assistant managing director responsible for the running of the company's vessels was the alter ego of the company and that the radar problem merited his personal attention. Also that a contributory cause of the collision was the master's total lack of sense of urgency of the problem posed by radar navigation in fog, which should have been instilled into him from the highest level, but was not. In these circumstances the Court ruled that the owners of the vessel were guilty of actual fault and could not, therefore, limit their liability. That ruling was upheld in the Court of Appeal.

So was a new facet of the interpretation and effect of the words "actual fault or privity" thrown into relief, to be followed many years later in an important ruling of the House of Lords in the case of the *Marion* in which the effect of the words were considered in relation to the supply and maintenance of up-to-date charts on board ships, which ruling delivered by the House left without doubt that that duty rested firmly and squarely with the owners of the vessel and should not be left in the hands of the master. The ruling of the Court made it clear that a casualty arising out of such failure on the part of the owners of a vessel would most likely be regarded as actual fault or privity and so deny the owners the right to limit liability under the provisions of Section 503 of the Merchant Shipping Act, 1894 and subsequent amending Acts.

What happend in the case of the *Marion,* was that the vessel dropped anchor off Hartlepool because of the unavailability of a berth at Teeside where she was due to load a cargo. When, some days later, a berth became available, she attempted to weigh anchor but was unable to do so because the anchor had fouled the pipeline which carried oil from the Ekofisk Field through Tees Bay to Teeside. As a result of the anchor fouling the pipeline and as a result of the efforts to haul it up, severe damage was caused to the pipeline giving rise to claims by various oil companies amounting to over $25,000,000. The owners of the *Marion* commenced an action for a declaration that they were entitled to a decree of limitation of liability under the provisions of the Merchant Shipping Acts, on the ground that the fouling of the anchor and the consequential loss and damage arose without their actual fault or privity.

This was again a case of the vessel being owned by one limited company, Grand Champion Tankers, Ltd., and the management of the vessel being delegated to another limited company, Fairfield-Maxwell Services Ltd. In this connection the Court found that the person whose fault would constitute, as a matter of law, the actual fault of the owners of the *Marion* was the managing director of Fairfield-Maxwell Services.

The immediate cause of the damage to the pipeline was the negligence of the master of the *Marion* in navigating by reference to a long obsolete chart on which the pipeline was not shown, leading him to let go his anchor in a place where, if he had been aware of the presence of the pipeline, as he would have been if he had navigated by reference to an up-to-date chart, he would never have done.

In contesting the right of the owners of the vessel to limit liability, the claimants submitted that the owners of the vessel had failed to discharge the burden of proof upon them to show that there had been no fault on the part of the managing director of Fairfield-Maxwell Services which contributed to the damage to the pipeline. Firstly it was said that the owners of the vessel had not proved that the managing director had a proper system for ensuring that charts and other nautical publications on board the *Marion* (a) were not obsolete or superseded or (b) if current, were kept corrected and up-to-date at all times. Secondly, it was submitted that the owners had not proved that there had been no fault on the part of the managing director in failing to ensure that that there was brought to his notice a document received by Fairfield-Maxwell Services from the Liberian Marine Inspectorate and known as a Safety Inspection Report, relating to an inspection a year before the casualty, which stated amongst other things that navigational charts for trade of vessel corrections were omitted for several years.

In delivering judgment and upholding the decision in the Court of Appeal that the owners of the vessel had not established that the casualty was caused without their actual fault or privity, the House of Lords said that it was the duty of the managing director of Fairfield-Maxwell Services to ensure that an adequate degree of supervision of the master of the *Marion,* in so far as the obtaining and keeping of up-to-date charts were concerned, was exercised by himself or by his subordinate managerial staff each of whom was fully qualified to exercise such supervision, and that in so far as the managing director failed to perform his duty in this respect such failure constituted in law actual fault of the owners of the vessel.

The Court found, amongst other things, that there were two actual faults of the owners, firstly in the failure of the managing director of Fairfield-Maxwell Services to have a proper system of supervision in relation to charts and secondly in failing, when he made a departure to Greece, to give his subordinate managerial staff instructions with regard to the matters about which he required to be kept informed which were sufficiently clear, precise and comprehensive, and that the owners of the vessel could not establish that these two faults did not contribute to the damage to the pipeline. *(Lloyd's Law Reports — 1983 — Vol. 2-156. House of Lords 1984 — Vol. 2-1).*

The case of the *Covent Garden* in which the owner of a steam drifter sought a decree of limitation of liability under the provisions of the Merchant Shipping Act, 1894, in respect of the claim by a widow of a member of the crew of the drifter when he fell overboard and was drowned is also of interest here. It seems that in the course of the voyage this crew member was instructed by the master of the vessel to secure the mizen sail to the boom, and it was alleged that he was required, in order to carry out the master's orders, to stand on the canvas cover of a dinghy. Owing to the breaking of a defective rope the man fell overboard and was drowned. In the liability proceedings the Court found that the man met his death owing to a breach of duty on the part of the owner of the drifter or his servants.

The owner of the drifter then sought to limit his liability under the provisions of Section 503 of the Merchant Shipping Act, 1894, and in finding that the owner was so entitled to limit his liability the Court said that although an owner was liable in law because of the failure of his servants to exercise a reasonable care, or because of a breach of duty owed by him to his servants to provide a safe system of work, he was not precluded from limiting his liability under the Act unless it was shown that he was personally negligent or, having properly delegated his duty to his servants, had failed to appoint competent servants. The Court found no evidence in this case of personal neglect of the owner and held that he was entitled to a decree of limitation of liability. *(1952 — 1 — Lloyd's Law Report — 266).*

These cases have been selected by the author from the many others illustrating the nature of the burden upon the owners of a vessel to discharge the burden of proof upon them that such casualty as may have arisen took place without their actual fault or privity and was not contributed to by any fault on their part.

● In the event that the required number of States ratify the Convention on Limitation of Liability for Maritime Claims 1976, Schedule 4 of the Merchant Shipping Act, 1979 will later become activated and the words "personal act or omission" will take the place of the words "fault or privity". (See notes under "Outlook for the future".)

CHAPTER II

"Alter Ego"

The person who may be found to don the mantle of the shipowner

LEGAL history has it that the expression "alter ego" was first used, in relation to application for a decree of limitation of liability under the provisions of the Merchant Shipping Act, 1894, by Counsel in the classic case of *Lennard's Carrying Company Ltd. v. Asiatic Petroleum Company Ltd.* And it would be helpful to the reader to run over, in the first place, a brief history of the events giving rise to that action, which was not brought with a view to limitation of liability under Section 503 but with a view to avoiding complete liability under Section 502 of the Act. Since the owners of the vessel were unable to prove that the loss of the cargo resulted without their fault or privity within the meaning of the Act, there was no entitlement to a plea for limitation of liability under Section 503.

The vessel concerned was the *Edward Dawson* which, at the time of the events leading to the action in this case, was under time charter to the Anglo Saxon Petroleum Company, under which charter she loaded a cargo of benzine at Novorossisk in Russia for carriage to Rotterdam. Whilst in the course of her voyage, and before she reached the English Channel, the two centre furnaces were completely salted up so that they had become useless, and two tubes in the boilers had burst.

Shortly after passing Dover the vessel encountered a strong north-westerly gale with heavy seas and when she was off the Dutch coast she hove to and set her head against the gale to prevent herself from being driven on to the lee shore, but she went aground because of insufficient power. She was unable to get off and was subjected to heavy bumping causing benzine to get loose from the tanks and get into the furnaces with the result that the ship went on fire and the cargo was lost by reason of the fire. The Court found that the vessel was unseaworthy.

The managers of the shipowning company were another limited company, John M Lennard & Sons Ltd., and the managing director of that company, John M. Lennard, who was the registered managing owner of the ship, was the person who took the active part in the management of the vessel on behalf of the owners. The Court said that he knew, or had the means of knowing, of the defective condition of the boilers but gave no special instructions to the captain or the chief engineer regarding their supervision and took no steps to prevent the ship going to sea with her boilers in an unseaworthy condition.

The owners of the vessel sought the benefit of Section 502 of the Act which provides immunity for the owner of a vessel for loss of cargo caused by fire, subject to the loss resulting without the actual fault or privity of the owners of the vessel. The Court said that in such a case as this the fault or privity is the fault or privity of somebody who is not merely a servant or agent for whom the company is liable but somebody for whom the company is liable because his action is the very action of the company itself. It is not enough, the House of Lords stated in finally deciding the issue, that the fault should be the fault of a servant in order to exonerate the owner; the fault must be also one that is not the fault of the owner or a fault to which the owner is privy. It was held that the owners had failed to discharge the onus which lay upon them of proving that the loss happened without their actual fault or privity.

The Act does not use the words "alter ego" but says "owners". Section 503, as amended by subsequent legislation, provides that the "owners of a ship . . . shall not, where . . . without their actual fault or privity . . . any loss or damage is caused to any property . . . through the act or omission of any person (whether on board the ship or not) in the navigation or management of the ship . . . be liable in damages beyond the following amounts. . . ."

Bearing in mind that those parts of the Act relative to the limitation of the liability of the owner of a vessel for damage caused by such vessel, are primarily concerned with the protection of the owner against the negligent acts of his agents or servants, and that limitation of liability under the Act will be granted provided that the loss or damage was caused without the actual fault or privity of the owners of the vessel, the fault or privity must be the fault or privity of somebody who is not merely a servant or agent for whom the company owning the vessel is liable, but somebody for whom the company is liable because that person's action is the very action of the company itself. It is now commonly accepted that it is not enough that the fault should be the fault of a servant in order to exonerate the owner; the fault must be one which is not the fault of the owner, or a fault to which the owner is privy.

Hence, in cases where a limited company is concerned, it has for a long time been the practice to find who should be regarded as the "alter ego" of that company, in establishing whether or not the loss or damage caused by the vessel arose without the actual fault or privity of the "owners" of the vessel, and once again reference is made to the case referred to above, when, amongst other things, the Court provided guidance on this problem, and since when it has been generally recognised that the words "actual fault or privity" infer something personal to the owners of the vessel, something blameworthy in them, as distinguished from constructive fault or privity such as the fault or privity of their servants or agents. In the case of a limited company this raises the question of who is the "alter ego" of the company.

However, the words "actual fault" are not confined to affirmative or positive acts by way of fault, and if the owner be guilty of an act or omission to do something which he ought to have done, he is no less guilty of an "actual fault" than if the act had been one of commission. In order to avail himself of the statutory defence, he must show that he himself is not blameworthy for either having done or omitted to do something or been privy to something. It is not necessary to show knowledge. If he has means of knowledge which he ought to have used and does not avail himself of such knowledge, his omission to do so may be a fault and he cannot then claim the protection of Section 503 of the Act, and the owner may find that he has no shelter behind the person who may be, within the meaning of the law, his "alter ego".

For a clear demonstration of this, the reader should refer to the case of *The Lady Gwendolen,* a vessel owned by a company primarily concerned with brewing and with shipowning very much ancillary to brewing, namely Arthur Guiness, Son & Co. (Dublin) Ltd. This vessel was constantly running between Dublin and Liverpool on a tight schedule and the casualty giving rise to the legal action in this case arose out of the master of the vessel proceeding at excessive speed in dense fog in the Crosby Channel in the River Mersey on a voyage from Dublin to Liverpool laden with a cargo of stout. She struck an anchored vessel, the *Freshfield* and as a result of the collision the *Freshfield* sank with her cargo.

The owners of *The Lady Gwendolen* accepted liability for the collision but asked for a decree of limitation of liability. This application was opposed by those having claims against the owners of the vessel, on the ground that the collision did not occur without the actual fault or privity of the owners of the vessel, in that they laid down a schedule for *The Lady Gwendolen* which could not be kept without at times proceeding at excessive speed with no or not sufficient regard for whether it was safe to do so in the prevailing weather or traffic conditions. Further, that they failed sufficiently or at all to instruct the master of *The Lady Gwendolen* to place considerations of safety above those of keeping to his schedule or alternatively if they did so instruct him they took no sufficient steps to see that such instructions were carried out, and failed to ensure that the master of the vessel knew that the owners did not expect him to arrive at his destination on time regardless of weather or traffic conditions.

The main submission, amongst the many others put forward by those opposing the application for a decree of limitation of liability, was that the owners of the vessel failed sufficiently or at all to instruct the master of the vessel not to proceed at excessive speed in fog or alternatively, if they did instruct him, they took no (or no sufficient) steps to see that such instructions were carried out. Also that the owners failed to ensure that the master and/or the mate of the vessel were properly instructed in the use of radar including the fact that the presence of radar on board the vessel did not make it safe for a vessel to proceed at full speed in dense fog.

As mentioned above, the shipowning side of the business of the owners of *The Lady Gwendolen* was a subsidiary to their main activity. But, when the application for a decree of limitation of liability came before the Court, the Court said that they were, nevertheless, shipowners and as such had the same obligations and the same rights as other shipowners whose principal business is shipowning.

Evidence was given that the master of the vessel habitually proceeded at excessive speed in fog and that the owners of the vessel knew of his addiction to speed in fog, which they should have restrained, and that the owners took no action to direct the master in the proper use of radar.

9

The question then arose as to who was the "alter ego" of the company. The Court said that these owners or any other owners could not divest themselves of their obligations by delegating these to salaried officials and that there must be a limit as to how far this or any other company may divest itself personally of such shipowning obligations as are of a fundamental or highly important nature.

In the view of the Court the radar problem was one of such serious importance as to merit the personal attention of the owners, and it was the duty of the "alter ego", whom the Court found to rest in the assistant managing director of the company, who was responsible, *inter alia,* for the company's vessels. It was held that the proper function and use of radar in fog was never considered by the assistant managing director or in fact anyone else, and that the total lack of urgency of the problem posed by radar navigation in fog in the master of the vessel was a contributory cause of the collision. This sense of urgency and importance should, the Court said, have been instilled in the master from the highest level, and this failure to do so rendered the owners of the vessel guilty of actual fault, the fault of omission, and the application for a decree of limitation of liability was refused.

That was the ruling of the Admiralty Division and the case then came before the Court of Appeal, when the Court virtually reiterated the ruling of the lower Court and said that the owners of the *Lady Gwendolen,* in their capacity as owners of the vessel, were to be judged by the standard of conduct of the ordinary reasonable shipowner in the management and control of vessels. The Court said that the primary concern of a shipowner is the safety of life at sea, and properly manned and properly navigated ships, and that in so far as high speed in fog was encouraged by radar, the installation of radar required the particular vigilance of shipowners through, in this case the "alter ego", namely the assistant managing director, who was responsible, *inter alia,* for the running of the ships and who had failed in that vigilance.

It was held that the owners of the vessel had failed to prove that the collision occurred without their actual fault or privity and the appeal against the ruling of the lower Court denying the application for a decree of limitation of liability was dismissed.

One of the prime considerations in the safe navigation of a vessel is the availability on board the vessel of up-to-date corrected charts, which must be used, and any obsolete or out-of-date charts should be segregated from current charts or destroyed. It has now been firmly established that the duty concerning the fulfilment of this requirement lies squarely with the owner of the vessel and/or the alter ego of the company. In the case of a vessel being owned by one limited company and managed by another limited company, then that duty will fall upon the managing company and/or the alter ego of that company. It is not sufficient that the company shall have taken steps to ensure that the vessel is navigated by a fully competent master and have placed upon him, or left to him, the duty of keeping the vessel provided with current charts or charts corrected up-to-date and ensured that only such charts are used in the navigation of the vessel.

Any views to the contrary that may have been held in the past have now been completely dispelled by the ruling of the House of Lords in the case of the *Marion* which vessel, a tanker, came to anchor off Hartlepool in a position about 2.7 miles east of the Heugh. Four days later when she attempted to weigh anchor she found that she could not do so because, as was subsequently discovered, her anchor had fouled a pipeline running from the Ekofisk Field through Tees Bay to Teeside. The pipeline was severely damaged and its owners and other companies (mostly oil companies) lodged claims for the loss they had suffered, which amounted to a figure exceeding U.S.$25m. The owners of the vessel sought a decree of limitation of liability under the provisions of Section 503 of the Merchant Shipping Act, 1894, as amended by the Merchant Shipping (Liability of Shipowners and Others) Act, 1958.

The immediate cause of the damage and loss was the negligence of the master navigating the vessel with uncorrected charts upon which the pipeline was not shown. The owners of the vessel sought to limit their liability on the ground that the damage to the pipeline was caused without their fault or privity. The Judge in the Admiralty Court found in favour of the owners of the vessel, on the ground that the provision and maintenance of the charts, including their correction, being matters incidental to navigation, fell within the sole responsibility of the master, and that the owners were justified in relying on the master to ensure that the vessel was provided with adequate and up-to-date charts of the areas to which the vessel traded. That ruling was short-lived as when the case came before the Court of Appeal the Court held, *inter alia,* that where there was a particular hazard of accident due to failure to have up-to-date charts on board which was or ought to have been known to the shipowners, then it was their duty to ensure that their vessels were supplied with the latest up-to-date charts, and it was not sufficient for the owner to rely on his master to obtain the necessary publications and information for the purpose of navigation.

In dismissing the appeal against the ruling of the Court of Appeal, the House of Lords went somewhat further and said, *inter alia,* that in considering whether a shipowner, in an action for a decree of limitation of liability under the Merchant Shipping Acts, had discharged the onus of showing that the loss or damage was caused without the fault or privity of the owner, it was no longer good enough to show that the shipowners had appointed a competent master and then left all questions of safe navigation (including obtaining, at their expense, all necessary charts and other nautical publications) entirely to the master.

The Court laid down three requirements with regard to charts which had to be fulfilled in order to ensure the safe navigation of the ship on the voyages undertaken by her, namely (1) the current versions of the relevant charts should be on board the vessel and available for immediate use; (2) any obsolete or superseded charts to be either destroyed or at least segregated from the current charts in such a way as to avoid the possibility of confusion; (3) the current charts should be either corrected up-to-date at all times or at least such corrections should be made prior to their possible use on any particular voyage.

The *Marion* was, in this case, being managed by another company, and it seems that the system of these managers with regard to charts was to make the master solely responsible for ensuring that these three requirements were fulfilled. The Court said that the managing director of the vessel's management company, the alter ego in this case, had a duty to ensure that an adequate degree of supervision of the master in the keeping of up-to-date charts was exercised either by himself or by a subordinate management staff, and that insofar as the managing director had failed to perform his duty in that respect, such failure constituted actual fault of the shipowners. And as the shipowners had therefore failed to establish that the damage to the pipeline had occurred without their actual fault, they were refused a decree of limitation of liability.

The question arises as to whether the alter ego of a company can be held to be personally liable to an injured party and, if so, whether such a person can limit his liability under the provisions of Section 503 of the Merchant Shipping Act, 1894. Some guidance on this issue may be found by reference to the case of the *Radiant (Lloyd's Law Reports — 1958 — 2 — 596)* which arose out of the injuries suffered by the skipper of a motor fishing vessel after it had gone aground in the Thames Estuary at night and was taken in tow by a sister ship.

After the vessel, the *Radiant,* had gone aground, her engine was put astern but it was found impossible for her to refloat herself in the prevailing conditions of wind and tide. Shortly afterwards a sister ship, the *Margaret Hamilton,* which had been following about two miles astern of the *Radiant,* came up with her and remained near in order to tow her off when the tide rose.

At about 19.00 hours the tide had risen sufficiently to refloat the *Radiant,* which by then had lost her rudder and was badly leaking due to the pounding of the vessel on the sand. At this time there were no lights on board the *Radiant* except her navigation lights, so that her decks were in darkness. No lights at all were burning on the *Margaret Hamilton* due to her battery having been discharged and her dynamo belt having come adrift, added to which her gear box had jammed so that she could not go astern.

It was not safe in the prevailing conditions for the *Margaret Hamilton* to stop her engine, and, since by reason of those matters she could only take off her way to a limited extent by throttling back her engine, it was inevitable that a snatch should occur when she took the *Radiant* in tow. It was in these circumstances that she approached the *Radiant.*

The tow rope was of poor quality and as soon as it became taut it broke and the operation was repeated twice using similar rope from the *Radiant* with the same result. Wire was then coiled on deck by the skipper of the *Radiant,* thrown by him to the *Margaret Hamilton* and on that ship made fast. But the *Radiant* skipper's legs became caught up in the coil of wire as the *Margaret Hamilton* took up the slack, resulting in his feet being amputated.

Thereafter the skipper of the *Radiant* claimed against the owners of the vessels, and also the managing director of the company, alleging that his injuries were caused by the unseaworthiness of both vessels due to their defective equipment and negligent navigation of the *Margaret Hamilton.* (As regards the claim against the owners of the vessels and as regards their plea for limitation of liability, this has been dealt with elsewhere in this book in the chapter dealing with "Collisions between tug and tow".)

It was held that the effective causes of the accident were (1) the grounding of the *Radiant* due to the negligent navigation of the *Margaret Hamilton;* (2) the inadequacy of the ropes; (3) the defective condition of the vessel's gear box; and (4) the absence of a deck-light on the *Radiant.* It was also held that the skipper of the *Radiant* was not negligent in allowing his feet to be caught up in the wire.

As regards the claim against the managing director who, admittedly, was the alter ego of the company, the Court said that he knew or had the means of knowing of the defects in the vessels which contributed to the accident and that there was, on his part, a failure of management, in that no adequate provision was made for periodical inspection. Accordingly the Court ruled that the owners of the vessel had failed to discharge the burden of proving that the accident occurred without their actual fault or privity and could not therefore limit their liability.

The Court then went on to say that an officer of a company, whether a director or other official in the service of the company was, in law, capable of being a joint tortfeasor with the company itself, which would also be vicariously responsible for his wrongful acts. It was held that the skipper of the *Radiant* had discharged the burden upon him of proving that the managing director was a party to sending the vessels to sea in an unseaworthy condition, and that his injury resulted from that condition. It was therefore held that the managing director was liable personally and that there was no question of his limiting his liability under the provisions of Section 503 of the Merchant Shipping Act, 1894.

Judgement in this case was delivered by Lord Justice Willmer but the ruling in that case must be tempered with the ruling of his Lordship in the Court of Appeal in the case of the *Anonity (Lloyd's Law Reports 1961 — 1-203 and 1961 — 2 — 117)* and his Lordship's comments must be borne in mind in relation to the foregoing. Referring to his ruling in the case of the *Radiant,* he said that it was true that that was a case in which on its own particular facts he had come to the conclusion that a personal action lay against the managing director of a company on the same facts as actual fault or privity was found against the company. But, he said, he was not prepared to accept that this must necessarily be so in all cases, and the question of whether an injured claimant could successfully bring a personal action against a member of a company, whose conduct is held to amount to actual fault or privity of the company within the Merchant Shipping Acts, must depend on whether, in the particular case, the relationship of "neighbours" in the eye of the law is established.

The case of the *Neapolis II (Lloyd's Law Reports — 1980 — 2 — 369)* gave rise to this problem of the alter ego in relation to the question of the right of the owners of a wharf or dock to limit their liability, under the provisions of Section 2 of the Merchant Shipping (Liability of Shipowners and Others) Act, 1900, in respect of the damage suffered by the vessel whilst at a wharf situated on the River Neath at or near Briton Ferry, the wharf being leased to the operators of the wharf who sought to limit their liability in respect of the damage suffered by the vessel whilst at the wharf.

A more detailed account of the events leading to the claim by the owners of the *Neapolis II* against the operators of the wharf will be found in the chapter in this book covering "Dock owners' and wharf owners' rights to limitation of liability ...". But it will suffice to say here that this vessel arrived with a phosphate cargo in Neath Harbour on the morning of September 18, 1977. She reached a point some 40 ft distant out into the river off the wharf, when she grounded. Attempts to refloat her proved unsuccessful and she remained aground in the same position until the evening of September 25, 1977.

On that evening she refloated but, because no pilot was available in this compulsory pilotage area, the vessel was winched to her final position by the crew under the direction of the master. There had been very heavy rain on September 24 and 25, with the result that as the tide fell after the evening high-tide there was the discharge from an outfall of some considerable force and volume which was being obstructed by the *Neapolis II* resulting in a scoured depression in the bed of the river which left a substantial portion of the vessel's length amidships unsupported and this lack of support caused damage to the vessel as she grounded.

It was common ground that the discharge from the culvert outfall, at any rate at times, made it hazardous to berth across it, this being fully appreciated by the operators of the wharf and for this reason they had given the pilot and the boatman instructions that vessels were not to be berthed in way of the white line marking the outfall. But no clear warning notices of the danger had been put up to indicate to visiting vessels that they should not be moored in way of the white line.

In holding that the wharf operators were not entitled to a decree limiting their liability under the provisions of Section 2 of the Merchant Shipping (Liability of Shipowners and Others) Act 1900, the Court said that it was negligent not to put up clear warning notices and found that had such warning notices been put up in a position clearly to have been seen, the *Neapolis II* would have seen that it was necessary to berth further upstream than she did so as to avoid the danger and would no doubt have done so.

As this absence of notices and the existence of the danger were well known to the managing director of the wharf operators, who was the directing mind or "alter ego" of the operating company in this connection, the Court said that it had to follow that if such absence was causally connected with the damage to the vessel, as it was, the wharf operators could not rely on the limitation of liability in the 1900 Act.

● In the event that the required number of States ratify the Convention on Limitation of Liability for Maritime Claims 1976, Schedule 4 of the Merchant Shipping Act, 1979 will later become activated and in this event the question as to who may be regarded as the alter ego may need to be reconsidered, because the term "personal act or omission" will replace the present term "fault or privity". (See notes under "Outlook for the future".)

CHAPTER III

Collisions between ships

Some guidelines as to circumstances in which shipowners may or may not succeed in proving absence of their actual fault or privity.

IN almost every case of a collision between two vessels, the cause will be found to be negligent navigation on the part of either one or both of the vessels concerned. In the event of dispute between the owners of the vessels as to the question of responsibility for the collision, if this cannot be reconciled amicably, the Courts may be called upon to settle the issue, in which event the Courts will apportion liability between the respective owners.

In either event, when liability has been agreed or apportioned by the Court, the owners of the vessels will assess the extent of the damages due from them and should it prove to be the case that the amount of their liability exceeds a sum calculated upon the tonnage of their vessel under the provisions of the Merchant Shipping Act, 1894 and subsequent amendments, they will seek to limit their liability under the provisions of Section 503 of the Act. This is subject to the owner of the vessel concerned being satisfied that the collision occurred without his actual fault or privity, for it is only when he is able to discharge the burden of proof upon him in this respect that a plea to the Court for a decree of limitation of liability will succeed.

The owners of the other vessel may well study the evidence as to the cause of the collision (or, in the case of legal proceedings to establish liability, the findings of the Court as to the cause of the collision) and reach the conclusion that the collision did not occur without the actual fault or privity of the owner. In this event the owner of the vessel claiming damages will seek to deny the right of limitation of liability being sought by the owners of the other vessel, upon the ground that the damage or loss resulting from the collision was not caused without the actual fault or privity of the owner of such vessel.

The emphasis must of course be placed upon the fact that in order to resist a plea for limitation of liability the owner of a vessel seeking to deny the owners of the other vessel the right of a decree of limitation of liability must bring some sort of prima facie showing that the *owner* of the vessel was personally at fault in the events leading to the collision, as distinct from the faults or failures on the part of his servants or agents, for the reason that one of the prime objects of the provisions for the limitation of liability contained in the Merchant Shipping Act, 1894, is a measure of protection for the owner of a vessel from the results of negligence of his agents or servants, but not of the negligence of the owner himself. In the case of a limited liability company, the owner, within the meaning of the Act, may be regarded as what is commonly termed the alter ego, which is the subject matter of a separate chapter in this volume.

The navigation of a ship, in the process of carrying goods or persons from one port to another, is so much in the hands of her master, officers and crew and so much out of the hands of or control of the owners of the vessel that it is almost inconceivable, since in the ordinary course of events the owner or owners of the vessel will not be on the bridge, that it could be levelled against the owner or owners of the vessel that they were guilty of some fault or privity in the case of collision with another vessel arising out of negligence in navigation. But the case of *The Lady Gwendolen* had the effect, amongst many others, of destroying any such myth.

This vessel, whilst on a voyage from Dublin to Liverpool, collided with and sank the motor vessel *Freshfield* whilst she was at anchor in the Crosby Channel, a buoyed approach to the River Mersey. The collision was due to the complete and inexcusable negligence of the master of *The Lady Gwendolen* in continuing his course in that channel at full speed in dense fog, and while so doing, failing to have manned, or himself effectively observed and made use of, the radar installation with which his ship was equipped.

The owners of *The Lady Gwendolen* had no alternative but to admit liability but they brought an action to limit their liability, for the damage caused by the collision, under the provisions of Section 503 of the Merchant Shipping Act, 1894. There was no question but that they were entitled to a decree limiting their liability if they were able to establish that the loss or damage, though caused through the act or omission of any person, whether on board the ship or not, in the navigation or management of the ship, was so caused without their actual fault or privity.

The owners of the vessel were not on board at the time of the collision and the ship was under the control of the master who was on the bridge in charge of the navigation with one able-seaman at the wheel; hence the plea of the owners of the vessel that they were entitled to limit their liability under the provisions of the Act because, they submitted, the collision occurred without their actual fault or privity. But they found that they were unable to discharge the onus of proof upon them to show that the collision in fact occurred without any fault or failure on the part of the owners of the vessel.

The main case made against the owners of *The Lady Gwendolen* by the owners of the *Freshfield* and others who had suffered loss or damage by reason of the collision, was that, in submitting that the collision did not occur without the fault or privity of the owners of *The Lady Gwendolen* and that they were not, therefore, entitled to limit their liability under the provisions of Section 503 of Merchant Shipping Act, 1894, this highly negligent navigation on the part of the master of the vessel was not an isolated act of negligence, but that over the years of his service in this ship the master had navigated at excessive speed in fog.

According to the vessel's logs she had on many occasions on her voyages to and from Dublin and the Mersey, either Liverpool or Manchester, maintained full speed in fog, and the master of the vessel had to admit that he had done so. It seems that the marine superintendent of the owners had perused the vessel's logs in the performance of his duty but had failed to detect the master's habit of navigation in such dangerous circumstances; or, if he did so, or if he suspected it, he had failed to warn the master and to seek to deter him from this practice or to take any steps to see that the regulations were complied with. Also he had failed to inform his employers, who throughout seemed to have been unaware of the risks that the master of the ship was taking.

The obvious sources of fault lay with the master and the marine superintendent and on the face of the matter it would seem obvious that the actual fault leading to the collision was that of the servants of the owners of the vessel. Why then was it found by the Court that the owners were not entitled to a decree of limitation of liability, on the ground that there was actual fault of the owners or at least a failure on their part to prove no actual fault or privity?

The reason was that the Court found that the assistant managing director was the alter ego (as regards the expression 'alter ego' see the chapter in this book on that matter) of the company owning the vessel and the radar problem merited his personal attention. The High Court ruled that a contributory cause of the collision was the master's total lack of sense of urgency of the problem posed by radar navigation in fog, which should have been instilled in him from the highest level, and that, therefore, the company owning the vessel were guilty of actual fault. The application for a decree of limitation of liability was declined.

The owners of *The Lady Gwendolen* appealed against the decision of the High Court but the appeal was dismissed, the Court of Appeal commenting that, although the main business of the company owning the vessel was that of brewers, in their capacity as shipowners they were to be judged by the standard of conduct of the ordinary reasonable shipowner in the management and control of vessels; that the primary concern of a shipowner was the safety of life at sea, and that that involved a seaworthy ship, properly manned and safely navigated.

The Court said that insofar as high speed in fog was encouraged by radar, the installation of radar required particular vigilance of shipowners through the person who was responsible, in the capacity of the owners, for the running of the ships, in this case the assistant managing director, and that the company owning *The Lady Gwendolen* had failed in that vigilance and had failed to consider or appreciate the problems that had arisen through the use of radar and to impress their master with the gravity of the risks he was taking, and that that was a contributory cause of the collision. It was held that the company owning the vessel had failed to prove that the collision occurred without their actual fault or privity, and that they were not entitled to a decree of limitation of liability.

Supervision of navigation

It is well established that it is upon the owners of a vessel involved in a collision who seek to limit their liability in respect of the loss or damage caused by the collision, to prove that the collision occurred without their actual fault or privity, or that if there was fault on their part that that fault was not causative of the collision. That point is well illustrated in the case of the collision between the vessel *Garden City* and the vessel *Zaglebie Dabrowski*, the law case that followed being known by the short title *The Garden City (Lloyd's Law Reports — 1982 — Vol 2 — 382)*.

The collision in this case occurred shortly before noon in the North Sea, the visibility at the time being much restricted by fog and as a result of the collision the *Garden City* sank in deep water with almost the whole of her cargo but there was no loss of life. In the proceedings to establish liability, the Court found that both ships were seriously to blame for bad radar look out, excessive initial speed in fog and failure to take off way before a close-quarters situation developed. The *Zaglebie Dabrowski* was further found at fault in altering course to starboard on sighting, all these faults being found causative of the collision.

Although the initial speed of both ships was found to be excessive, that of the *Zaglebie Dabrowski* (at $12\frac{1}{2}$ - 13 knots) was higher than that of the *Garden City* (at $10\frac{1}{2}$ - 11 knots) and the Court found that in the circumstances the *Zaglebie Dabrowski* was substantially more to blame than the *Garden City,* the former vessel being held to be 60 per cent to blame and the latter 40 per cent.

The loss suffered by the owners of the *Garden City* and her cargo was substantial and considerably more than the loss suffered by the owners of the *Zaglebie Dabrowski* who now sought to limit their liability under the provisions of Section 503 of the Merchant Shipping Act, 1894. Those making the claims against the owners of this vessel resisted the plea for a limitation of liability on the grounds that the collision did not occur without the actual fault or privity of the owners of the *Zaglebie Dabrowski,* in that (1) they failed to ensure that the vessel was manned with competent officers (2) failed to ensure that there was a system providing for two officers to be on the bridge when the vessel was navigating in fog (3) failed to supervise and check how their vessels were navigated, especially in fog, in regard to (i) speed and (ii) use of radar. The burden was now on the owners of the vessel to prove that the collision and subsequent loss occurred without their actual fault or privity.

Although the Court found that there was fault for which the owners of the *Zaglebie Dabrowski* were vicariously liable, in that the master of the vessel had failed to arrange for a replacement when he left the bridge some 50 minutes before the collision, having been on the bridge continuously for over eight hours, and the third officer had set the radar to the six mile range instead of the 12 mile range, and the initial speed of the vessel should have been no more than 8 - 9 knots, since visibility was no more than $\frac{3}{4}$ of a mile, there was nothing to indicate actual fault or privity on the part of the owners of the vessel.

The Court then made an important observation to the effect that the top management of every shipowning corporation ought to institute a system for the supervision of navigation and detection of faults, and that in this case the fact that the organisation regulations did not provide that supervision of navigation was one of the tasks which was the responsibility of the director of technical and investment affairs, and did not provide that it was one of the tasks of the chief navigator, was not causative of the collision since both the director and the chief navigator were well aware of their responsibilities.

There was a system of inspections in existence by which after every voyage the chief navigator or one of his staff would go on board every vessel of the company when it returned to a home port and although the Court thought that it was not perfect it was nevertheless adequate. There was a system providing for two officers to be on the bridge when the vessel was navigating in fog but the master did not keep to it. The Court found that there was no fault by any superior of the master and third officer in this respect. The chief navigator was found to be at fault but the Court found that this was not the actual fault of the owners of the vessel since the chief navigator and his staff were not the directing mind of the company either in practice or under the company's constitution.

The Court concluded by finding that there was no fault on the part of the director-general or the director in that they did what it was reasonable for the owner of a large number of ships to do, *i.e.*, they appreciated the navigational problems posed by the use of radar in fog and impressed the urgency of such problems upon the masters of their vessels and took steps to ensure as far as they reasonably could that their vessels were safely navigated in fog. It was therefore held that the owners of the *Zaglebie Dabrowski* were entitled to a decree of limitation of liability under the provisions of Section 503 of the Merchant Shipping Act, 1894.

The *Lady Gwendolen* and *Garden City* cases, taken together, will provide, as regards navigation of vessels in fog, an interesting study because on the one hand there is well illustrated the nature of the failures that a shipowning company may be found guilty of, of such a nature that might result in their being denied a decree of limitation of liability, whereas on the other hand there is illustrated that by the institution of a system for the supervision of navigation and detection of faults the shipowning company may be successful in proving they were not guilty of actual fault or privity and successfully apply for a decree of limitation of liability.

Manning of the vessel relative to limitation

One of the prime considerations and duty of a shipowner or a shipowning company, is that of ensuring that the vessel is properly manned. And if there be any actual fault or privity on the part of an owner or company in this respect which leads to collision with another vessel or contributes to the cause of the collision, then, in the event of the owner or owners seeking to limit their liability, in respect of the damage done as a result of the collision, under the provisions of the Merchant Shipping Act, 1894, their plea for a decree of limitation of liability would most likely fail on the ground that the owner or owners had not been able to discharge the burden of proof upon them that the collision occurred without their actual fault or privity.

An example of this situation is provided by the proceedings before the Admiralty Division in the case of the *Dayspring (Lloyd's Law Reports — 1968 — 2-204)* which vessel collided with the motor tanker *Auspicity* off the Point of Ayre, Isle of Man. At the material time of the collision a watch was being kept on the bridge of the trawler *Dayspring* by her mate and the wheel was in the hands of a deckhand. In those circumstances the mate observed the *Auspicity* on the port bow of the trawler distant between two and three miles and heading round to the Point of Ayre in the opposite direction to the trawler. The mate then left the bridge without warning the helmsman of the presence of the *Auspicity*.

It seems that thereafter, as the vessels reached the turning point at the Port of Ayre, the helmsman of the *Dayspring*, without orders, brought the *Dayspring* rapidly to port at a time when the *Auspicity* was hidden from his view because of the flare of the bow. The *Dayspring* struck the port side of the tanker about amidships, resulting in the *Auspicity* and her cargo suffering considerable loss and damage.

In the proceedings to establish responsibility for the collision, the owners of the *Auspicity* claimed damages from the owners of the *Dayspring* and, in the result, the Court found that the *Dayspring* was at fault for altering course to port when the vessels were about one cable apart and were in a position to pass safely port-to-port, and for not sounding a signal. The vessel was also held to be at fault in that no look-out was kept on board. As regards the *Auspicity*, the Court said that if she had sounded signals on the two occasions when she starboarded, they would have aroused those on board the *Dayspring*, and that that failure contributed to the collision. The Court apportioned the blame as to the *Auspicity*, one-fifth, and as to the *Dayspring*, four-fifths.

The owners of the trawler then claimed a decree of limitation of liability under the provisions of the Merchant Shipping Act, 1894, on the grounds that the collision occurred without their actual fault or privity, and was the result of negligent navigation by those on board the trawler. The owners of the *Auspicity* contended that the collision did not occur without the actual fault or privity of the owners of the *Dayspring* in that they failed to ensure that there should always be a look-out on deck in a position where he could see ahead clearly, and in that they permitted the helmsman to serve on board the vessel as helmsman when he was unfit by reason of defective vision.

When the issue came before the trial Court, evidence was given that the "skipper's standing orders" displayed in the wheelhouse provided, *inter alia*, "Always ensure that there are at least two men in the wheelhouse". Those orders also required that a logbook should be kept but that rule was not observed. Evidence was also given that in twelve Formal Investigations between 1947 and 1961 (the collision in this case occured in November, 1961) one of which involved the trawler *Winnmarleigh* which was owned by the same owners as the *Dayspring*, the Courts had commented on the dangers inherent in the undermanning of bridges on trawlers.

The Court reached the conclusion that the skipper and mate of the *Dayspring* knew that as a general rule the vessel should not be under way in charge of the helmsman alone, but that it was not clear that they regarded that as a rule to be strictly observed. Also that comments by the Court of Formal Investigation into the *Winnmarleigh* case should have alerted the owners to the importance of having a logbook regularly kept, and that they were at fault in failing to insist on the keeping of proper logbooks.

Among other things, the Court said that something much stronger than the notice in the wheelhouse was required and that there was a reasonable likelihood that if a proper logbook had been kept the mate would not have

20

left the wheelbase, and that there was a causal link between that fault and the casualty.

In the result the Court found that the owners of the trawler had not proved that the occurrence took place without their fault or privity and were, therefore, not entitled to a decree of limitation of liability. The Court also held that there was no fault on the part of the owners of the *Dayspring* in not submitting their deck hands to an eye-test, adding that it could not be said that the helmsman's failure to observe the tanker was a contibutory cause of the collision. Further, that even if the defective eyesight of the helmsman had been known to the owners of the trawler or to the skipper of the vessel, it was not negligence to let him take the wheel, since keeping a look-out formed no part of his duties at the time.

Uncertificated officers and local rules

Perhaps one of the most interesting cases arising out of questions as regards the manning of a vessel, in relation to the question of the right of the owners of a colliding vessel to limit liability in respect of the damage done by their vessel in the collision, was that of the *Empire Jamaica (LLR-1955-1-50. Court of Appeal 1955-2-109. House of Lords 1956-2-119)*. Briefly outlined, the events leading to a legal dispute which was eventually determined in the House of Lords, were that whilst navigating in the Java Sea early on the morning of September 1, 1951, the steamship *Empire Jamaica* came into collision with the motorship *Garoet*. The owners of the *Empire Jamaica* eventually admitted sole responsibility for the collision, but brought an action for limitation of liability under Section 503 of the Merchant Shipping Act, 1894.

In their statement of claim they admitted that the collision and the damage consequent thereon were caused by improper navigation and/or management of their vessel, but said that the collision occurred without the owners' actual fault or privity. At the time of the collision the *Empire Jamaica* was carrying a certificated master, a certificated first mate and two other officers who were not certificated. These two uncertificated officers were a Mr. Sinon, who figured largely in the proceedings and who was described in the ship's particulars of engagement as "chief boatswain", and a Chinese officer who was described as "third officer". The Court accepted that the vessel carried these three men to perform the duties as mates and that they were in fact employed and paid as such. The contention of the owners was that in all the circumstances of the case they had good reason to believe that Mr. Sinon was fully competent to perform the functions which would fall upon him including the keeping of a watch, and thus the collision occurred without their actual fault or privity.

The owners of the motorship *Garoet* contended that the evidence produced by the owners of the *Empire Jamaica* failed to prove this allegation and, in addition to criticising the evidence, they alleged also that the owners of the *Empire Jamaica* were in breach of the provisions of Section 4 of the Hong Kong Merchant Shipping Ordinance 1899, as amended. The owners of the *Empire Jamaica* denied that they were in breach of the Ordinance but that if they were then that breach had no casual connection with the collision.

The Ordinance, as amended, provided, *inter alia,* by Section 4(3) that, "Every British ship ... shall, when leaving any port in the Colony, be provided with officers who possess certificates of competency ... according to the following scale (a) in any case, with duly certificated master; (b) if the ship is of one hundred tons or upwards, (the *Empire Jamaica* was 3,538 tons gross), with at least one officer besides the master holding a certificate not lower than that of only mate, or second mate in the case of a sailing ship of not more than 200 tons; (c) if the ship carries more than one mate, with at least the first and second mates duly certificated."

The collision occurred on a clear but dark night and the two ships were on nearly opposite courses. The *Empire Jamaica* was proceeding at her full speed of 10 knots and her navigation was then in charge of an uncertificated officer, Mr. Sinon, who was acting as second officer. The owners of the *Garoet* contested the claim for limitation of liability put forward by the owners of the *Empire Jamaica,* on the ground that in having an uncertificated man in charge of the navigation at the time of the collision the *Empire Jamaica* was not properly manned.

It was held in the trial Court that the non-provision of the requisite number of certificated officers was not of itself enough to render an owner guilty of fault or privity in relation to a casualty subsequently occurring, and that the undisputed evidence being that Mr. Sinon was a fully competent seaman, no causal connection had been shown between the fact of having no certificate and the fact of his negligent navigation. The Court ruled that the owners of the *Empire Jamaica* were entitled to a decree of limitation of liability.

On appeal, the Court of Appeal ruled that the owners of the vessel had discharged the onus of proving that in all the circumstances of the case they had good reason to believe that the man that they engaged in the capacity nominally of chief boatswain, but actually and in practice as second mate, was fully competent to perform the functions which would fall upon him. The Court dismissed the appeal against the granting of limitation of liability, and the issue then came before the House of Lords when the granting of the decree of limitation of liability was upheld, on the ground, *inter alia,* that even if the owners of the *Empire Jamaica* were in breach of the Hong Kong Ordinance in appointing an uncertificated man as second mate, that breach neither caused nor contributed to the collision. The Court said that the owners of the vessel had good reason to believe that Mr. Sinon was fully competent to perform the functions which would fall upon him when acting as second mate, and that it had also been shown that the responsible authority would have granted permission to employ this man as second mate merely upon compliance by the owners of the vessel with Section 4 (3) (b).

Maintenance of steering machinery

The case of the *Otterdal,* which vessel was responsible for the sinking of another vessel, the *Tarbet,* brings into relief the retribution that may follow upon failure to ensure that the steering machinery of a vessel is properly maintained. The *Otterdal* came into collision with the *Tarbet* in the River

Mersey as the result of which the latter vessel sank. The owners of the *Otterdal* sought to limit their liability for the collision and the loss of the other vessel, under the provisions of the Merchant Shipping Act, 1894. The application for a decree of limitation was contested by the owners of the *Tarbet* and others who had suffered by reason of the sinking of the vessel.

When the case came before the trial Court to establish liability for the collision it was held that the collision was caused by a fault in the steering machinery of the *Otterdal*, a fault which existed at the time the vessel sailed. She had therefore sailed in an unseaworthy condition and the question that now arose, in the limitation of liability proceedings, was whether that unseaworthiness, that defective condition of the steering gear, existed without the actual fault or privity of the owners of the vessel.

It seems that a correspondence extending over many months between the owners of the vessel and the master showed that the tinkering with the steering machinery such as the master and certain advisers did was no good, and that leaving it to the master and the chief engineer was of no use, and that a thorough overhaul was necessary. But it seems nothing was done and the vessel continued to sail despite doubts about the manoeuverability of the vessel in crowded waters.

Trouble of this nature, making the risk of collision clear, had not so far resulted in collision until the *Otterdal* struck the *Tarbet* in the River Mersey. But the Court said that there was no justification for the owner, after the history of the steering gear, allowing the ship to sail on that voyage without being assured that something thorough had been done to the steering gear or that new gear had been installed. The Court said that the fact of the matter was that the owner took a chance, the same as he had done on other voyages, but unfortunately for him on this voyage the chance that he took turned out to be wrong, and he was not entitled to a decree of limitation of liability, in that the owners of the *Otterdal* had wholly failed to discharge the burden upon them to show that the collision, and the damages that flowed from the collision (of which the defective steering gear was the cause) occurred without their actual fault or privity. The Court of Appeal upheld this ruling. (LLR — *1920 — 4-414 and LLR — 1920-5-368).*

Before leaving this chapter, reference must be made to the case of the *Annie Hay (LLR-1968-1-141),* which, whilst not arising out of the sinking of a commercial vessel but a motor yacht, nevertheless is one of importance in the consideration of the interpretation of the Merchant Shipping Acts. What happened here was that the owner of the *Annie Hay* had agreed to provide his vessel as a patrol boat during a power-boat race and he acted as master of the vessel and navigator. Whilst so performing in Falmouth Harbour his vessel struck the yacht *Rosewarne,* causing her to sink, the loss resulting substantially from the negligent navigation on the part of the owner of the *Annie Hay,* who sought to limit his liability under the provisions of Section 503 of the Merchant Shipping Act, 1894, as amended by the Merchant Shipping (Liability of Shipowners and Others) Act 1958.

Relevant to the plea for a decree of limitation of liability were the provisions of Section 3 (2) of the Merchant Shipping (Liability of Shipowners and Others) Act, 1958, which provides that ". . . in relation to a claim arising from the act or omission of any person in his capacity as master or member of the crew or (otherwise than in that capacity) in the course of his employment as a servant of the owners or of any such person as is mentioned in Subsection (1) of this section, (a) the persons whose liability is excluded or limited as aforesaid shall also include the master, member of the crew or servant, and, in a case where the master or member of the crew is the servant of a person whose liability would not be excluded or limited apart from this paragraph, the persons whose servant he is; and (b) the liability of the master, member of the crew or servant himself shall be excluded or limited as aforesaid notwithstanding his actual fault or privity in that capacity, except in the cases mentioned in Paragraph (ii) of Section 502 of the said Act of 1894."

The owner of the *Annie Hay* said that the claims of the owner, the charterers and sub-charterer of the *Rosewarne,* four passengers on the *Rosewarne* and one passenger on board the *Annie Hay,* in respect of the loss they suffered as a result of the collision, were made against him in his capacity as master and that in accordance with the natural meaning of the words in Section 3 (2), he was entitled to limit his liability. The claimants submitted that the owner of the *Annie Hay* was not entitled to limit his liability, contending that, in the context of Section 3 (2), persons referred to were employees, and that, in the context of the Act, persons entitled to limit were employers in respect of their vicarious liability providing they were not personally at fault and employees who could limit although personally at fault.

The Court decided that the owner of the *Annie Hay* was entitled to limit his liability under the provisions of the Merchant Shipping Acts, for the reasons, amongst other things, that in Section 3 (2) the words "any person in his capacity of master" were wide enough to include the owner of this vessel, and that there was no need to give the words a narrower meaning as had been contended by the claimants.

The case of the *Truculent* concerned an action in which the Admiralty sought limitation of liability under the provisions of the Merchant Shipping Act, 1894, in respect of material damage, loss of life, and personal injury caused to civilian personnel lost in the submarine *Truculent* or on board the Swedish steamship *Divina* as a result of the collision between the two vessels. Liability for the collion was admitted on behalf of The Admiralty.

The collision occurred at night and both vessels were exhibiting lights. The *Divina* was exhibiting masthead and side-lights, and, in addition, being laden with petroleum, was exhibiting a red light in accordance with Petroleum Spirit in Harbours Order, 1939. The *Truculent* was exhibiting a white steaming light, mounted on top of the periscope housing above the conning tower, and also side-lights mounted on each side of the conning tower. During the course of the hearing, evidence was given that it would be practically impossible in the case of a submarine to fit a steaming light that would conform exactly with the requirements of Article 2 (a) of the Collision Regulations.

The Court ruled, however, among many other matters, that the fact that it was impracticable for submarines to comply with the requirements of the

Collision Regulations with regard to the positioning of lights afforded no answer to the charge that the steaming light of the *Truculent* constituted a breach of the Regulations. It was held that the submarine was at fault in exhibiting what were misleading lights, and that such lights in fact misled the *Divina* and were a contributory cause of the collision. Also that the provision of navigation lights rested with a responsible member of the Board of Admiralty, who must, therefore, be found privy to the fault of the submarine in exhibiting improper lights and accordingly the claim of the Admiralty for limitation of liability had to be dismissed. *(1951 — Lloyd's Law Reports — Vol. 2 — 308.)*

An interesting issue arose also out of the negligent navigation of the barge *Alde*. The barge *Tom Tit* was forced into collision with the steamship *Ascania*. The owners of the *Alde* sought to limit their liability under the provisions of Section 503 of the Merchant Shipping Act, 1894, in respect of the resulting damage. At the time of the collision the work of navigating the *Alde* was being assisted by the use of a capstan on board the grain sucker *Turbo*.

The owners of the *Ascania* and the *Tom Tit,* and other interests, contended that the collision was due in part to the negligence of individuals working a capstan on board the grain sucker, and that consequently the owners of the *Alde* were not entitled to limit their liability at all or, alternatively, they were only entitled to limit their liability upon the basis of the combined tonnage of the *Alde* and the *Turbo*.

The Court ruled that since the damage was caused solely in the course of the navigation of the *Alde,* the owners of this barge were entitled to limit their liability upon the basis of the tonnage of the *Alde (LLR — 1926 — 25 — 419.)*

Further examples of collision liabilities will be found by reference to the chapters on "Collisions arising out of fault or neglect in pilotage", "Collisions between tugs and tugs and tow", and "Security or bail provided by arrest of vessel".

CHAPTER IV

Damage to property ashore

The nature of the burden upon shipowners to prove absence of fault or privity

SECTION 1 of the Merchant Shipping (Liability of Shipowners and Others) Act, 1900 provides that the limitation of the liability of the owners of any ship set by Section 503 of the Merchant Shipping Act, 1894, in respect of loss of or damage to vessels, goods, merchandise, or other things, shall extend and apply to all cases where (without their actual fault or privity) any loss or damage is caused to property or rights of any kind, whether on land or on water, or whether fixed or movable, by reason of the improper navigation or management of the ship.

Before considering the effect of Section 1 of the Act of 1900, it is felt that it would be helpful to the reader to have in front of him certain provisions of Section 503 of the Merchant Shipping Act, 1894, namely Subsection (1) which provides that ". . . the owners of any ship, British or foreign, shall not, where all of the following occurrences take place without their actual fault or privity (that is to say) (a) where any loss of life or personal injury is caused to any person being carried in the ship; (b) where any damage or loss is caused to any goods, merchandise, or other things whatsoever on board the ship; (c) where any loss of life or personal injury is caused to any person carried in any other vessel by reason of the improper navigation of the ship; (d) where any loss or damage is caused to any other vessel, or to any goods, merchandise, or other things whatsoever on board any other vessel, by reason of the improper navigation of the ship; be liable to damages beyond the following amounts. (There then follows the limitation figures which are regulated from time to time by amendments to the Act.)

The events which followed upon the arrival of the vessel, *Athelvictor,* at Lagos on December 5, 1942, provided, amongst other things, an in-depth study of the above limitation of liability provisions. In this case, known as *The Athelvictor,* the owners of the vessel sought to limit their liability for damage caused by an explosion and fire. Petroleum spirit had escaped from the vessel because certain sea-valves were open and fire and explosion followed causing damage to other vessels, harbour installations and property, and, tragically resulting in 68 persons losing their lives and others being injured. The owners of the vessel accepted that such loss and damage was caused by the negligence of those on board the vessel but made application for a decree of limitation of liability under the Merchant Shipping Acts.

The claimants in the proceedings disputed that the owners of the vessel were entitled to limit liability, and contended that the damage done was not due to the negligent navigation or management of the ship, but to negligence in the management of the cargo. It was further argued that if the damage was caused by negligent management of the ship, no statutory authorities entitled the owners of the vessel to limit their liability in respect of loss of life in this case.

The Court reached the conclusion that the negligent failure of the ship's personnel to close the sea-valves did not amount to improper navigation of the ship and that, therefore, the shipowners were not entitled to limit their liability in respect of the life claims or personal injury claims. The Court, in considering the meaning to be given to the words "improper management of the ship" in a limitation action, was entitled to disregard the narrower construction put upon words in disputes arising under contracts evidenced by bills of lading, and in giving the words their ordinary and natural meaning, "improper management of the ship" included improper management of the ship's appliance (where, as here, they were fitted for ship and cargo purposes) and covered the negligence of the ship's personnel in the present case, and it was therefore held that the owners of the vessel were entitled to limit their liability in respect of the damage done to other vessels and to property ashore.

It is of interest that, in delivering that ruling, the Court was satisfied that, removed from the framework of an Act governing the mutual rights, obligations and immunities of shipowner and cargo owner, such as the Harter Act, or the Carriage of Goods by Sea Act, the ordinary and natural meaning of the words "improper management of the ship" covered improper management of the appliances of the ship, at any rate where, as in this case, such appliances were fitted both for ship's purposes and for cargo purposes.

The Court was satisfied also, by a careful examination of all the bill of lading cases, that the narrower construction placed upon these words in such cases was so placed because such construction was the only one which enabled proper effect to be given to the shipowners' obligation under the overriding Act to take care of the cargo entrusted to him. In this case the Court was not fettered by any such limiting considerations in construing the words "improper management of the ship" in the sections of the Merchant Shipping Acts with which the Court was concerned, and the Court took the view that none of these sections regulated the position as between shipowner and cargo owner or in any way governed their relationship. It was the view of the Court that occurring in the context which they did in this case, the words had a wider meaning than that which had been given to them in the bill of lading cases referred to above.

The comments of the Court in the case of the *Athelvictor* were adopted by the Court in the case of the *Anonity (LLR — 1961 — 1 — 203; Ct Appeal — 1961 — 2 — 117),* which arose out of a fire which broke out on an oil jetty at Thameshaven on April 14, 1955, when the vessel was lying at the jetty. As a result of the fire the jetty was destroyed, and installations and other property were damaged. It was accepted that the fire was caused by the negligence of those on board the *Anonity* in leaving the galley stove burning or smouldering at a time when it should have been turned off completely, thereby causing or allowing sparks to escape from the galley stack on to the jetty.

The owners of the vessel sought to limit their liability, contending that the negligence found constituted improper management of the vessel within the meaning of Section 1 of the Merchant Shipping (Liability of Shipowners and Others) Act, 1900, and that the fire and damage occurred without their actual fault or privity. They claimed a decree of limitation of liability.

The owners of the jetty and installations contended that the cause of the fire did not constitute improper management or navigation of the ship so as to permit the owners of the vessel to limit their liability under the provisions of the Act and contended that the fire and the damage caused by the fire were due to the actual fault or privity of the owners of the vessel, in that they failed, *inter alia,* to give clear or adequate instructions about the use of galley stoves on their ships when such ships were at petroleum installations, and failed to operate disciplinary checks upon the masters of their ships so as to make them properly responsible for the due observance of statutory prohibitions imposed in the interests of safety etc.

Dealing firstly with the question of whether the negligence causing the damage constituted improper management of the vessel within the meaning of Section 1 of the Act of 1900, the Court adopted what had been said by the Court in the case of the *Athelvictor (LLR — 1945 — 78 — 529)* to the effect that the ordinary and natural meaning of the words "improper management of the ship" covered improper management of the appliances of the ship at any rate where such appliances were fitted both for the ship's purposes and cargo purposes. In the opinion of the Court in this present case, causing or allowing sparks to escape from an oil-burning cooking stove, which should not have been burning at all while the vessel was at the jetty in question, was improper management of an appliance fitted solely for the ship's purposes and was therefore within the meaning of Section 1 of the Act of 1900. The Court found that there was a misuse of this appliance and that this misuse, which caused the fire and the damage, was caused by the improper management of the ship.

Then came the question of whether the fire and the damage occurred without the actual fault or privity of the owners of the vessel. In this connection the Court referred to what was said by the Court in the case of *Asiatic Petroleum Company v. Lennard's Carrying Company;* namely, that the words "actual fault or privity" inferred something personal to the owner, something blameworthy in him, as distinguished from constructive fault or privity such as the fault or privity of his servants or agents, but that the words "actual fault" were not confined to affirmative or positive acts by way of fault. If the owner is guilty of an act or omission to do something which he ought to have done, he is no less guilty of an "actual fault" than if the act had been one of commission.

In the opinion of the Court in that case, the owner, to avail himself of the statutory defence, must show that he himself is not blameworthy for either having done or omitted to do something or been privy to something. It was not necessary, the Court said, to show knowledge, and if he has the means of knowledge which he ought to have used and does not avail himself of them, his omission to do so may be a fault, and, if so, it is an actual fault and he cannot claim the protection of Section 1 of the Merchant Shipping (Liability of Shipowners and Others) Act, 1900.

The issue in the case of the *Anonity* turned upon whether adequate instructions had been given by the owners of the vessel to their servants with regard to the extinguishing of fires when the vessel was lying alongside an oil jetty. In the event, owners of the vessel failed to satisfy the Court that they had given adequate and proper notice prohibiting the use of galley fires at oil berths and their plea for limitation of liability therefore failed. The appeal against this ruling was dismissed in the Court of Appeal.

It seems that a notice to the masters of the vessels owned by these owners, issued some twelve months previously, specifically required the masters of vessels to bring an accompanying notice from the Purfleet oil installation to the immediate attention of their officers and crews, and the owners contended that having issued those instructions, they could not be held to have been guilty of any actual fault or privity in relation to this disastrous fire caused a year later which they submitted was due entirely to the fault of the master.

The Court of Appeal upheld the ruling of the Admiralty Court that the promulgation of this notice was not enough, which decision, the Court found, was sufficiently proved by the fact that the notice merely found its way on to the ship's file and was not seen again.

The case of the *Kathleen (LLR — 1925 — 22 — 80)* must receive a mention here too, in that she was involved in damage to the gates of a lock as she entered at excessive speed. The *Kathleen* was entering Barton Lock in the Manchester Ship Canal but when the engineroom received the order from the bridge for the engines to be put full astern, the engineer was unable to get any movement of the engines owing to jamming. In the result the vessel entered the lock at excessive speed resulting in the lock gates being carried away.

It seems that there had been two previous accidents of a similar nature, and when the owners of the vessel sought a decree of limitation of liability, in respect of the damage done to the lock gates, the Manchester Ship Canal Company opposed the claim on the ground that if the owners of the vessel had taken proper notice of the two previous accidents and had had a proper overhaul of the engines of the vessel, this casualty would not have occurred.

However, the Court granted a decree of limitation of liability and, in so granting the plea of the owners of the *Kathleen,* the Court said that if the defective condition of the engines was a contributory cause to the collision, that condition existed without the actual fault or privity of the owners of the vessel. As regards the meaning of actual fault or privity in the case of owners who are incorporated, the Court referred to the remark of Lord Justice Buckley in the case of *Asiatic Petroleum Co. v. Lennard's Carrying Company* when he said that "There must be something blameworthy on them, or an individual to whom they entrust their responsibilities, as distinguished from constructive fault or privity of their servants or agents."

The test question posed was, "Could it be said that the owners had nothing to do with it, and that only their servants . . . if any person, were to blame."

The accident in June, 1920, when the steamship *Countess (LLR — 1922 — 13 — 416),* while in the Mersey Docks, went ahead instead of astern with the result that she ran into and burst open the dock gates causing damage to a number of barges and other craft, some of which were sunk, later gave rise to some interesting issues under the provisions of Section 1 of the Merchant Shipping (Liability of Shipowners and Others) Act, 1900, and the effect of the act in relation to Dock Authority rules and regulations and, *inter alia,* priorities in a limitation action.

At the time of the accident, the Mersey Docks Acts Consolidation Act, 1858, was in operation, under which, by Section 94, it was provided that "... where damage shall be done to the Dock Board's property through the negligence of those in charge of any vessel, such vessel may be detained until the amount of the damage or a deposit for the estimated amount of the damage has been paid."

The *Countess,* which was holed and in a sinking condition, was towed into shallow water. After the accident and whilst the *Countess* was still afloat, the Mersey Docks Board marine surveyor certified that the vessel was in a sinking condition within the port of Liverpool and was an obstruction or impediment or danger to the safe navigation of the port, or was likely to become so, and the Dock Board claimed to detain the vessel under Section 94 of the Act. The owners of the vessel then patched her up and removed her to a graving dock where she was repaired.

The damage done to the property of the Dock Board amounted to £10,014, and the total claims amounted to around £80,000. The value of the *Countess* for limitation purposes amounted to £4,468. The issues between the parties reached the House of Lords when it was held that the owners of the vessel were entitled to limit their liability under the Merchant Shipping Acts and that the exercise by the Harbour Board of their statutory power to detain a ship doing damage to their property, conferred upon them a possessory lien. Further, that Section 1 of the Merchant Shipping (Liability of Shipowners and Others) Act, 1900 did not affect that lien beyond limiting the amount for which it could be exercised.

The Court concluded by saying that the Court, in distributing the statutory amount of the shipowners' liability amongst claimants, ought to have regard to the priorities as well as to the amounts of the claims and the Harbour Board were entitled to the whole of the fund in priority to the barge owners.

The case of the *Smjeli (LLR — 1982 — 2 — 74)* provides some interesting reading with regard to the question of damage to property ashore. The *Smjeli* was a tug which on January 13, 1977, was towing the dumb barge *Transporter III,* laden with several sections of an oil rig, from Rotterdam to Yugoslavia. She had reached a position about seven miles east of Dungeness when the towing hawser parted and the barge was then driven by a southerly gale towards the coast of Kent. At 20 00 hours on that day the barge ran aground some eight cables westward of Folkestone pier and damaged some groynes which were the property of the District Council of Shepway, resulting in some consequential loss and damage, in respect of which the council claimed damages against the owners of the tug and the barge, both of which were in the same ownership, the barge also constituting a ship under the provisions of the Merchant Shipping Act.

The owners of the tug and barge, a Yugoslav towing and salvage organisation known as Brodospas, admitted liability insofar as the damage had been caused by the sole and exclusive negligence of the master of the tug, but sought to limit their liability under the provisions of Section 503 of the Merchant Shipping Act, 1894, as amended, on the ground that the liability had arisen without their actual fault or privity. They also contended that their liability should be limited by reference to the tug alone, which had a gross registered tonnage of 946, the barge having a gross registered tonnage of 1,545. The Shepway Council, however, argued that if Brodospas were entitled to limit their liability, such liability should be calculated by reference to the tonnage of both vessels.

The Court ruled, *inter alia,* that if the council's claim had depended solely upon the allegation that the master of the tug was negligent in the navigation of the tug, the limit of the tug owners' liability would have been calculated by reference to the tug alone. But there was a cause of action against the barge which arose out of the negligent acts or omissions which occurred when making arrangements for the towage of the barge when she left Rotterdam, and a claim for damages would have been successful if a servant of the barge owner was guilty of those acts or omissions regardless of who owned the tug.

It was held that although the owners of the barge were not liable to damages beyond an amount calculated by reference to her tonnage, there was no reason why that liability should be limited to a lesser sum because the owners of the barge also owned the tug. Also that the council had a cause of action against the tug in that the master was negligent in his navigation of the *Smjeli* in causing or allowing the wire to part and in failing to seek shelter towards North Foreland and instead attempting to hold the tow in the Dover Strait.

CHAPTER V

Distinct and separate occasions

Where one damage succeeds another, can the second damage be claimed as negligence arising out of the first?

SUB SECTION (3) of Section 503 of the Merchant Shipping Act, 1894, provides that the owner of a vessel shall be liable in respect of every such loss of life, personal injury, loss of or damage to vessels, goods, merchandise "arising on distinct occasions" to the same extent as if no other loss, injury, or damage, had arisen. Simple enough, on the face of it, but in effect providing on occasions some contentious issues.

As illustrative of the position of the owner under this provision, four cases before the courts have been selected, those of the *Harlow,* the *Fastnet,* the *Ant* and the *Lucullite.* In the background of these cases is the question of whether the loss or damage caused by the owner of a vessel on the second occasion was caused by the negligence which caused the first damage or was there some intervening negligence causing the second?

The case of the *Harlow (LLR — 1922 — 10 — 66, 169, 244, 488)* gave rise to two separate legal actions arising out of the casualty when this tug, having in tow five of the barges belonging to the tug owners, came into collision with the steamship *Dalton* in the River Thames, causing considerable damage to the *Dalton.* The cause of the damage was the negligent navigation of the tug and on the barges and, in the event, the tug and one of the barges struck the *Dalton.* But another barge made fast to the colliding barge by her weight and momentum contributed to the damage.

The owners of the tug and barges sought a decree of limitation of their liability under the provisions of Section 503 of the Merchant Shipping Act, 1894, to an amount based on the tonnage of the tug or, alternatively, on the tonnage of the tug and the colliding barge. The owners of the *Dalton* contended that the owners of the tug and the barges in tow could not limit their liability on the tonnage of any of the barges because they were not "ships" or that, if "ships", they were not registered. However, that problem is dealt with in Chapter XI and it will suffice to say here that the owners of the tug and the barges were held to be entitled to a decree of limitation on the combined tonnage of the tug and the two barges.

There then followed the second action involving the tug. Her engines had been going at full speed and her steering gear had become jammed, and she had proceeded, after the collision with the *Dalton,* to make a turn in the river and hit another vessel. The owners of the tug *Harlow* now claimed that the damage payable to the owners of this vessel should come out of the same limitation fund established in respect of the earlier collision with the *Dalton.*

The question arose as to whether the latter casualty was a distinct and separate occasion from the first casualty, involving the steamship *Dalton*. The Court *(LLR — 1922 — 13 — 311)* found that the damage to the vessel concerned in the second casualty happened on the same occasion as the damage to the *Dalton* and that the damages payable to the vessel concerned in the second casualty must come out of the one limitation fund.

We proceed now to the case of the *Ant (LLR — 1924 — 19 — 211),* the owners of which vessel sought to limit their liability under the provisions of the Merchant Shipping Acts arising out of damage caused by a collision in the River Mersey between a barge which was in tow of the *Ant* and a steamship which was at anchor. After the collision between the barge and the steamship, the towing hook of the *Ant* parted and, wire having fouled her propellor, the *Ant* reported to another tug of considerable power that the barge was adrift, and then proceeded into dock. This second tug then went to the assistance of the barge and thereafter, the barge, in charge of this tug, collided with a wreck. Some time later the barge somehow got right across the river and drifted into collision with a staging belonging to the Birkenhead Corporation, causing much damage. The barge sustained damage herself, and the cargo being carried in the barge was also damaged.

The owners of the *Ant* sought a decree of limitation of liability claiming that the collision of the barge with the staging was a consequence of the earlier collision between the barge and the steamship, but the Birkenhead Corporation and the owners of the cargo on the barge disputed that the collision with the staging was a consequence of the collision between the barge and the steamship and contended that the two collisions occurred upon separate and distinct occasions, and that the loss in the cargo on the barge was due to the improper abandonment by the owners of the *Ant* of their contract to tow the barge.

The Court ruled that the collision of the barge with the Birkenhead staging was not caused by any separate or distinct act of negligence after the first collision and that whilst there was abundant time between the two collisions there was no opportunity negligently omitted by the *Ant*.

The cases of the *Lucullite (LLR — 1929 — 33 — 186)* and the *Fastnet (LLR — 1922 — 10 — 816)* provide a distinction, in that in both cases it was held that the first and second of the occasions giving rise to damage were separate and distinct occasions within the meaning of Sub-section (3) of Section 503 of the Merchant Shipping Act, 1894. Taking firstly the case of the *Lucullite,* the owners of this vessel sought to limit their liability in respect of collisions between their vessel and two other steamships.

The events giving rise to the proceedings in this case arose when the *Lucullite* was lying moored alongside and on the outside of another vessel. Owing to heavy wind and sea she was bumping against the other vessel causing considerable damage, and she therefore cast off and proceeded ahead into harbour. As she was doing so, her port bow struck the starboard quarter of another vessel which was lying ahead, doing such damage as to cause that vessel to sink.

In the proceedings for a decree of limitation of liability, the owners of the *Lucullite* contended that the damage done to the other vessels arose out of the same act of improper management on the part of those on the *Lucullite* in mooring where they did. On the other hand the owners of the two vessels which suffered damage by the collision between the *Lucullite* and their vessels, contended that the damage caused to their vessels arose on distinct occasions and did not arise from one and the same act of negligence on the part of the *Lucullite*.

On the issue coming before the Court, it was held that the second collision was not the necessary consequence of the first and that the two occasions of damage were separate and distinct. It was held, therefore, that the owners of the *Lucullite* could not succeed in bringing the two separate claims within the same limitation fund.

Reference should also be made to the case of the *Fastnet,* a tug which collided with another vessel under tow causing damage. At the same time, her tow came into collision with the pier-head. The owners of the vessel with which the tug collided recovered judgment against the owners of the tug in an action in which they and the owners of the tow were joined as defendants. The tug owners claimed a decree of limitation of liability.

The Court found that the tug owners were entitled to limitation in respect of the vessel with which their tug collided only, in that the master of the tug had time and opportunity to avoid the vessel after the tow was cast off, but failed to take proper action and occupied his time with action which was not the proper action to take for the vessel under tow, and it was held that therefore these were distinct occasions within the meaning of Sub-section (3) of Section 503 of the Merchant Shipping Act, 1894.

No doubt those responsible for the drafting of Sub-section (3) of Section 503 of the Merchant Shipping Act, 1894, had in mind the occasion when the owner of a vessel which had, by reason of negligent navigation, been involved in collision with more than one vessel of different ownerships at and around the same time, seeks to obtain a decree of limitation of liability based on the tonnage of his vessel to cover the claims arising out of the casualties caused to all such vessels.

It seems that to that extent Sub-section (3) will have achieved its object but, as the above cases will illustrate, the consideration of the problem of such right can be fraught with difficulty in deciding whether or not the various damages caused by the vessel are in fact separate and "distinct" occasions. The above cases will hopefully provide some guidance on the problem.

CHAPTER VI

Dock owners and wharf owners

Their rights to limitation of liability under the Merchant Shipping Acts.

SECTION 2 of the Merchant Shipping (Liability of Shipowners and others) Act, 1900, provides, in Sub-Section 1, that "... the owners of any dock or canal, or a harbour authority or a conservancy authority, as defined by the Merchant Shipping Act, 1894, shall not, where without their actual fault or privity any loss or damage is caused to any vessel or vessels, or to any goods, merchandise, or other things whatsoever on board any vessel or vessels, be liable to damages beyond an aggregate amount not exceeding £8 for each ton (this figure is constantly amended from time to time by amendments to the Merchant Shipping Act) of the tonnage of the largest registered British ship which, at the time of such loss or damage occurring, is, or within the period of five years previous thereto has been, within the area over which such dock or canal owner, harbour authority, or conservancy authority, performs any duties or exercises any power. A ship shall not be deemed to have been within the area over which a harbour authority or a conservancy authority performs any duty, or exercises any powers, by reason only that it has been built or fitted out within such area, or that it has taken shelter within or passed through such area on a voyage between two places both situated outside that area, or that it has loaded or unloaded mails or passengers within that area. ..."

Section (4) provides that "... for the purposes of this section the term "dock" shall include wet docks and basins, tidal docks and basins, locks, cuts, entrances, dry docks, graving docks, grid irons, slips, quays, wharves, piers, stages, landing places and jetties." Section (5) provides that "... for the purposes of this section the term 'owners of a dock or canal' shall include any person or authority having the control and management of any dock or canal, as the case may be."

The above provisions came under review in the case of the barge *Humorist (LLR — 1946 — 79 — 549)*, which, whilst berthed loading cargo alongside a wharf in the River Thames in March, 1943, took the ground on several tides and became waterlogged, her bottom having been set up due to the presence of some iron weights in the berth. The barge owners sued the owners of the wharf for damages, in which action they were successful, the Court holding the wharf owners liable in damages.

The owners of the wharf now sought to limit their liability in accordance with the provisions of the Merchant Shipping Act, on the ground that they were dock owners and were entitled to the protection of the Act and contending that the damage occurred without any actual fault or privity on their part. The Court ruled that the damage to the barge was sustained without the actual fault or privity of the wharf owners, and said that even assuming that the wharf owners' engineer was negligent, which the Court did not find, his act would merely be that of a servant.

It was held that the wharf owners' premises could properly be described as a "landing place", and, therefore, a "dock", for the purposes of the Act, and that the damage to the barge occurred within the area over which the wharfowners exercised control. It was therefore held that the wharf owners were entitled to a limitation decree based upon the registered tonnage of the largest vessel using the berth within the previous five years.

The case of the *Neapolis II* provides an interesting study of some further facets of the effect of Section 2 of the Merchant Shipping (Liability of Shipowners and Others) Act, 1900 on the liabilities of wharf owners and dock owners in respect of damage caused to a vessel whilst at its berth. The *Neapolis II* suffered damage by grounding whilst she was tied up against a wharf leased and operated by the defendants in these proceedings.

The wharf was known as the Ironworks Wharf and was situated on the River Neath at or near Briton Ferry. This wharf formed part of a longer wharf, the southern or downstream end of which was known as the Sand and Gravel Wharf. Between the two was a boundary wall or fence which formed a convenient datum for measurements along the wharf. The berths alongside were tidal and at low water the bed dried out from the foot of the quay wall for a distance of some 60 feet out into the river. Near the foot of the wall some 163 feet to the north of the boundary, there was a culvert outfall which discharged sewage and water from a stream and for a distance of some 10 - 15 ft on either side of a point vertically above the outfall. The top of the quay wall was painted white.

It seems that the discharge from the outfall made it hazardous at times to berth across it and although the pilot and boatman (this being an area of compulsory pilotage) had been given instructions not to do so, no warning notices had been put up to indicate that vessels should not be moored in way of the white line. The *Neapolis II* arrived at Neath Harbour on the morning of September 18, 1977, with a cargo of 2,500 tonnes of phosphates and had reached a point 40 ft distant out into the river off the wharf when she grounded. Attempts to refloat her were unsuccessful.

The vessel remained aground until the evening of the 25th September. On that day, at the upstream end of the wharf and facing upstream with her stern some 620 ft upstream of the boundary wall, was an old minesweeper, the *Corvo.* Moored at the Sand and Gravel Wharf and also facing upstream was a vessel called the *Murell.* She was some 200 ft long and was moored with her bow projecting some distance alongside the wharf. Between the stern of the *Corvo* and the bow of the *Murell,* and facing upstream was another vessel, the *Maycrest* which was some 195 ft long and was tied up alongside. The *Neapolis II* faced downstream, 40 ft from the quayside.

At high tide on that day the vessel lifted forward at 17 00 hours and aft at 17 25 hours. At 17 40 hours the *Murell* sailed and at 17 50 the *Maycrest* moved along the quay towards the Sand and Gravel Wharf where she was due to load. At 17 55 hours the *Neapolis II* was made fast in her final position, but because of the movements of the other two vessels no pilot was available to assist the *Neapolis II* and she was winched to her final position by her crew, under the direction of her master, with her stern about 350 ft and her stem about 85 ft from the boundary wall so that her stem was about 78 ft downstream of the outfall.

There had been some heavy rain on September 24 and September 25, after some very dry conditions, with the result that as the tide fell after the evening high tide, the discharge from the outfall was of considerable force and volume and, being obstructed by the presence of the *Neapolis II,* it scoured a depression in the bed of the river in way of her keel leaving a substantial part of her length amidships unsupported which caused the damage to the vessel by grounding.

It has been necessary to outline the above brief details of the events leading to the grounding and the damage to the *Neapolis II* to enable the reader to gain a proper impression of the finding of the Court arising out of the claim for damages by the owners of the vessel from the company who leased and operated the wharf. The principal dispute was whether the final berthing of the vessel was due to the negligence of the wharf operators or to the master of the vessel or both, the wharf operators also seeking a decree of limitation of liability under the provisions of Section 2 of the Merchant Shipping (Liability of Shipowners and Others) Act, 1900.

In the lengthy proceedings which followed, the Court found that it was negligent of the wharf operators not to put up clear warning notices and that had such notices been in position the *Neapolis II* would have seen that it was necessary to berth about 25 metres further upstream than she had done, so as to avoid the danger, and would no doubt have done so. Since the wharf operators were aware of the absence of the notices and the existence of the danger then, the Court said, it must follow that as such absence of notices and the existence of the danger were well known to the managing director of the wharf operators, it followed that such absence was causally connected with the damage and that, therefore, the wharf operators could not rely on the limitation of liability under Section 2 of the 1900 Act.

An interesting point came up for discussion in the case of the *Ruapehu (LLR — 1927 — 6 — 429),* namely whether the right of limitation of liability under the provisions of Section 2 of the Merchant Shipping (Liability of Shipowners and Others) Act, 1900, depended on geographical area or capacity. The case arose out of a fire which broke out in the *Ruapehu* whilst the vessel was undergoing repairs in the ship-repairers' own drydock at Blackwall, due to the negligence of the ship-repairers' servants. The ship repairers sought to limit their liability under the act in respect of the damage caused by the fire, but the owners of the vessel contended that the ship-repairers' liability arose out of their business as ship-repairers and not out of their business as dock-owners, and that, therefore, Section 2 of the Act of 1900 was not applicable.

The dispute finished up in the House of Lords where the Court, confirming the ruling of the Court of Appeal, held that the right of limitation of liability conferred upon dock-owners and others by Section 2 of the Merchant Shipping (Liability of Shipowners and Others) Act, 1900, was dependent on the area over which the dock-owners performed their duty and not in the capacity in which the dock-owners acted. It was also held, *inter alia,* that since, at the time of the accident the ship-repairers were using the drydock in the ordinary course of their business, they were entitled to limit their liability under Section 2 of the act.

This case was followed later by another, the *Ruapehu* (No. 2) (LLR — *1929 — 34 — 402)* when the meaning of the word "area" in Section 2 of the Act of 1900 came up for discussion and a ruling. The ship-repairers had two drydocks at Blackwall and the largest registered ship to enter either of them was the *Ruapehu,* but it seems that the ship-repairers were closely associated with another company which had a drydock at Falmouth which had taken larger vessels than the *Ruapehu.* The dispute that now arose was that whereas the ship-repairers contended that their liability should be calculated on the tonnage of the *Ruapehu,* the owners of the vessel contended that the limitation of liability should be based on the tonnage of the largest registered vessel drydocked at Falmouth.

The Court, without deciding whether the dock of an associated company might be taken into consideration, held that upon the true construction of Section 2 (1) of the Merchant Shipping (Liability of Shipowners and Others) Act, 1900, the word "area" meant that area over which the limiting dock-owner performed a duty or exercised a power and which contained the dock in which the damage occurred. It was further held that the drydock at Falmouth was in a different area from the dock in which the damage occurred. The Court ruled that the ship-repairers were entitled to limit their liability calculated on the tonnage of the *Ruapehu.*

In the case of the *City of Edinburgh,* a firm of ship-repairers sought to limit their liability under the provisions of Section 2 of the Merchant Shipping (Liability of Shipowners and Others) Act, 1900, in respect of an injury done to the vessel *City of Edinburgh* whilst she was undergoing repairs. At the time of the damage done to the vessel she was lying in the Hornby Dock which was the property of the Mersey Docks and Harbour Board whereas the ship-repairs were the owners of a dry dock at Garston.

The ruling of the Court of Appeal in this case was that the loss was in no way connected with the ship-repairers' dock at Garston and that the ship-repairers were therefore not entitled to a decree of limitation of liability under Section 2 of the Act of 1900. *(LLR — 1921 — 6 — 429.)*

● In the event that the required number of States ratify the Convention on Limitation of Liability for Maritime Claims 1976, some twelve months later Schedule 4 of the Merchant Shipping Act, 1979, will come into effect, and among the provisions of the Act is Article 2 paragraph 1 (a) which contains a special provision in regard to harbour works. (See notes under "Outlook for the future".)

CHAPTER VII

Management of ship

The responsibilities of the shipowner vis-a-vis the provisions of the Merchant Shipping Acts with regard to limitation of liability.

THE words "management of ship" are used quite prolifically in various branches of maritime law, but they have various intentions and meanings. For example, they are used in the Hague Rules for the purpose of relieving the carrier of goods by sea, covered by a bill of lading, from liability for loss or damage suffered by the cargo arising or resulting from act, neglect, or default of the master, mariner, pilot or the servants of the carrier, in the management of the ship. In the case of the Merchant Shipping Acts with reference to the question of the right of a shipowner to limit his liability in relation to damage done by his vessel ashore or afloat, fault in management has an entirely different connotation.

Under the provisions of the Merchant Shipping Acts, the shipowner must, in order to plead successfully for a decree of limitation in respect of the damage done to other property, ashore or afloat, by his vessel, discharge the onus of proof upon him to show that the damage was caused without his actual fault or privity and was not contributed to by such fault. In the event that the owner of the vessel is unable to bring sufficient evidence before the Court to make such a showing, he will be unsuccessful in obtaining a decree entitling him to limit liability under the provisions of the acts.

In this context there are two major requirements of shipowners, namely that they shall have properly supervised the navigation of their vessels (the subject of a separate chapter in this book) and that they should have instituted a proper system in the management and operation of their vessels, with particular reference to the supervision of navigation, the detection of faults and to giving adequate and proper notice to masters of certain dangers inherent in the operation of vessels at sea or in port. Any fault in these respects by the owners of a vessel will almost inevitably stand in the way of the owner from obtaining a decree of limitation of liability under the provisions of the Merchant Shipping Acts, for the reason that it has long since been laid down that it is not enough that the fault or neglect leading to the casualty involving damage by the owners' vessel to other property should be the fault of a servant; the fault must also be one which is not the fault of the owners of the vessel or a fault to which the owners are privy.

In this connection reference has to be made to the alter ego of the company who may be charged with, or regarded as responsible for such matters as navigation and safety, but any fault on the part of that somebody may be regarded as the fault of the shipowners or shipping company itself.

When the shipowners are a limited company and they have appointed another limited company to operate or manage their vessels, then the Courts will regard any fault in the management of a vessel by the managing company as a fault of the owners of the vessel themselves, and the same considerations as above will apply in respect of such faults by the managing company or their alter ego.

For an appreciation of what all this means it is proposed in the first place to examine briefly that time-honoured case of the *Edward Dawson,* otherwise known as *Lennard's Carrying Company Ltd. v. Asiatic Petroleum Company Ltd.,* which arose out of the loss of a cargo of benzine caused by the unseaworthiness of the vessel by reason of the defective condition of her boilers. Whilst the action in this case arose out of the submission by the owners of the *Edward Dawson* that they were exempt from liability under the provisions of Section 502 of the Merchant Shipping Act, 1894, and was not a plea for limitation of liability under the provisions of Section 503 of the Act, the case has a particular and important place in this volume because it turned upon the question of whether the loss of the cargo occurred without the actual fault or privity of the shipowner and laid down some very important guidelines on this question which are still followed to this day. The case also provided the origin of the expression 'alter ego' in relation to the person in the shipowning company upon whom rests the responsibility for the operation of the company's vessels.

Briefly, the facts leading to the casualty were that after the vessel loaded a cargo of benzine at Novorossisk in the Black Sea for delivery at Rotterdam, the unsatisfactory condition of her boilers soon became manifest. The boilers leaked salt water into the central furnaces, the furnaces became silted up with salt so that their capacity was diminished and the vessel was unable to develop such power as was desirable in the event of her encountering heavy head weather.

Whilst off the Dutch coast she encountered a gale and set her head against that gale to prevent herself being driven on to a lee shore. But she was so driven, and first grounded on the Botkill Bank and then again in the mouth of the Scheldt and was unable to get off. As a result of her bumping, the benzine got loose from the tanks, began to get into the furnaces and the vessel went on fire, the cargo of benzine being lost. The Court found that the vessel was unseaworthy when she left Novorossisk by reason of defects in her boilers.

The shipowners were a limited company and the managing owners were another limited company, John M. Lennard & Son, who were responsible for the management of the vessel. The managing director, Mr. Lennard, took the active part in the management of the ship on behalf of the owners of the vessel and the Court found that he was the alter ego of the company and that he knew, or had the means of knowing, of the defective condition of the boilers, but gave no special instructions to the captain or chief engineer regarding their supervision and took no steps to prevent the vessel going to sea with her boilers in an unseaworthy condition. In these circumstances the Court found that the owners had failed to discharge the onus which lay upon them of proving that the loss happened without their actual fault or privity.

That case was decided in the House of Lords in 1915, since when there have followed many legal actions arising out of the right of a shipowner to limit liability under the provisions of the Merchant Shipping Acts, which have been contested by those suffering damage to their property for which the shipowner is liable, when the duties of a shipowner in relation to the management of the vessel have been adjudicated upon. The following cases have been selected by the author as representative and illustrative of the nature of those duties and the burden of the onus of proof upon the shipowner of the proper discharge of those duties and obligations, that is if the owner is to be successful in seeking entitlement to limitation of liability under the provisions of the Merchant Shipping Acts.

Perhaps the most important case decided since the *Edward Dawson* is the most recent, namely the case of the *Marion,* decided on May 17, 1984, which, like certain other cases, also involved questions of supervision of navigational matters. Here we are concerned with the question of what action a prudent shipowner, in the management and operation of a vessel, should take to ensure that the vessel is supplied with up-to-date and corrected charts.

The *Marion* dropped anchor over a submerged oil pipeline and in her efforts to weigh anchor she so severely damaged the pipeline as to give rise to claims by a number of oil companies to the tune of some $25m. The owners of the vessel brought an action to limit their liability to a sum of £982,292.06, on the ground that the incident occurred without their actual fault or privity within the meaning of the words in Section 503 of the Merchant Shipping Act, 1894, as amended by the Merchant Shipping (Liability of Shipowners and Others) Act, 1958. The action was contested by the claimants who claimed that the cause of the fouling of the pipeline by the anchor of the *Marion* did not occur without the fault or privity of the owners of the vessel.

In the first place it should be mentioned that, as in the case of the *Edward Dawson,* the owners of the ship were a limited company and the company responsible for the managing of the ship were also a limited liability, so that in such a case the Court would look to the managing company when considering whether the owners were guilty of fault or privity. In the case of the *Marion* the owners of the vessel had delegated the management and operation of the vessel wholly to an English company, recorded in short as F.M.S.L., and the person whose fault would constitute as a matter of law was the managing director of this company.

The master of the *Marion* had fouled the pipeline because he was unaware of its presence due to the fact that he was navigating with an out-of-date and uncorrected chart, due, it was alleged, to the managing director failing to have a proper system of management for ensuring that the charts and other nautical publications on board the vessel were not obsolete or superseded, or, if still current, were kept up-to-date at all times. Also that the managing director was at fault for failing to ensure that during his absence from office there was brought to his attention a document from the Liberian Marine Inspectorate, known as a Safety Inspection Report that stated, amongst other things, that navigational charts for trade of vessel corrections had been omitted for several years.

The House of Lords ruled that it was the duty of the managing director, in the management of the vessel, to ensure that an adequate degree of supervision of the master of the *Marion,* so far as the obtaining and keeping of up-to-date charts were concerned, was exercised either by himself or by his subordinate managerial staff, and that insofar as the managing director failed to perform his duty in this respect such failure constituted in law actual fault of the owners of the vessel, and the owners therefore failed to persuade the Court that they were entitled to a decree for limitation of liability.

A forerunner in the legal decisions laying down management responsibilities of shipowners in the supply of information to their vessels was the case of the *Norman (LLR — 1960 — 1 — 1)* which was finally decided in the House of Lords. Briefly stated the facts were that whilst this vessel, a trawler, was at sea her owners were given new information as to dangers in the area in which the *Norman* was likely to be navigated but the owners, in their management and operation of the vessel, did not pass this information on to their vessel because they were of the opinion, *inter alia,* that to have wirelessed information to the vessel would have been an unnecessary departure from their normal practice and also because it related to an area known by the skipper of the trawler to be unsafe.

In the event, the vessel struck an uncharted rock and was lost together with 19 out of 20 members of her crew whose dependents brought an action against the owners of the vessel who sought to limit their liability under the provisions of Section 503 of the Merchant Shipping Act, 1894. The House of Lords said that there was a duty on the owners of the vessel to communicate this new information to the vessel and that this was a fault, and that the owners had failed to prove that that fault did not contribute to the foundering of the vessel and the owners had failed to prove that the loss of the vessel did not arise without their actual fault or privity.

The management and operation of small ships has special considerations for the owners of such vessels and in this connection the attention of the reader is brought to the case of the *England (LLR — 1972 — 1 — 375. Court of Appeal — 1973 — 1 — 373)* which was damaged when she was in collision with the *Alletta,* a vessel of some 500 tons, in the River Thames in the hours of darkness early one morning. The *Alletta* was held to be 80 per cent to blame for the collision and brought an action to limit her liability under the provisions of the Merchant Shipping Acts. This application for a decree of limitation of liability was contested by the owners of the *England.*

The owners of the *England* contended that the collision was caused or contributed to by the actual fault or privity of the *Alletta's* managing owner in failing to ensure that the master of the vessel did not navigate in the River Thames without a pilot, and failed to ensure that there were copies of the relevant river by-laws on board the vessel. The Court of Appeal declined to grant a decree of limitation of liability and said that the managing owner should have foreseen that without specific instructions, the master, however competent, might fail to have the Port of London River by-laws available or fail to study them, and that in the management of the vessel the managing owner was under a duty at least to give specific instructions to the master that, in trading to the Port of London, he must have available a copy of the by-laws.

It had been submitted to the Court that it was a practice that owners expected their masters to obtain for themselves copies of the regulations for foreign ports, but the evidence before the Court did not establish the existence of such a practice. The Court also said that it should be regarded as a managerial responsibility to provide a copy of the by-laws or to instruct the master to see that there was a copy on board, and that the owner of a vessel is not entitled simply to rely upon the master to get the necessary regulations or otherwise instruct himself.

It was therefore found that the owners of the *Alletta* had failed to disprove that the absence of the by-laws on board the vessel was a contributory cause of the collision, and that accordingly they were not entitled to a decree of limitation of liability.

This problem of the supply of information to a vessel, in the course of her day-to-day management, and the potential danger that may follow any neglect in this respect, and in the event of a casualty, may deny the owners of a vessel the right of limitation of liability under the provisions of the Merchant Shipping Acts, was thrown into relief by the extraordinary circumstances leading to the case of the *Clan Gordon (LLR — 1923 — 16 — 367)*, which vessel overturned and sank in fine weather. She had sailed with two of her ballast tanks full of water, but when two days out, the captain, for the purpose of trimming the vessel more by the stern in order to give the vessel more freeboard and so give her more speed, ordered the water to be pumped out of the tanks. When the tanks were nearly empty, and while the course of the ship was being altered, she heeled over, gradually turned turtle and became a total loss.

It seems that a year or so earlier a sister ship of the *Clan Gordon* overturned and sank in fine weather in very much the same way and, consequent upon the loss of this vessel, instructions were prepared by the builders for the guidance of masters as to the loading of this class of ship. These instructions, which were sent to the owners, included a direction that when this class of ship (referred to as a 'turret ship') was loaded with a homogeneous cargo, as was the case with the *Clan Gordon,* the water ballast tanks should be full. These instructions, for some reason or other, were never communicated to the captain by the owners.

The owners of the vessel were held liable for the loss of the cargo but put forward a plea for limitation of liability under Section 503 of the Merchant Shipping Act, 1894, which plea eventually finished up in the House of Lords when it was decided that the owners were not entitled to a decree of limitation of liability for the reason that they had failed to show that the loss occurred without their actual fault or privity.

Another classic example of the nature of the duties of the shipowner in ship management, relevant to limitation of liability under the provisions of the Merchant Shipping Acts, in recent years, is the case of the *Lady Gwendolen* which arose out of that vessel proceeding at speed in the River Mersey in conditions of dense fog when she collided with and sank the motor vessel *Freshfield.* Her owners were the brewers Arthur Guinness, Son & Co., who accepted liability for the damage and loss done by the collision but brought an action for the limitation of their liability under Section 503 of the

Merchant Shipping Act, 1894, on the ground that the loss and damage, though caused by the negligence of the master of the vessel, was caused without their actual fault or privity.

In this case the owners failed to obtain a decree of limitation of liability, and the Court said that although the owners' main business was that of brewers, in their capacity as shipowners they were to be judged by the standard of conduct of the ordinary reasonable shipowner in the management and control of vessels, and that in so far as high speed in fog was encouraged by radar, the installation of radar required particular vigilance of shipowners through the person who was responsible, in the capacity of the owners, the alter ego, in this case an assistant managing director, who was responsible for the running of the company's ships.

It was held that the owners had failed in that vigilance and had failed to consider or appreciate the problems that had arisen through the use of radar and had failed to impress upon their master the gravity of the risks he was running in navigating his vessel at high speed in fog, and that that was a contributory cause of the collision, and that the owners had therefore failed to prove that the collision occurred without their actual fault or privity.

Before proceeding to further cases in which the owners of vessels have failed in an action to obtain a decree of limitation of liability because of, amongst other things, a failure in the management of their vessels, it is proposed to digress for a moment for the purpose of illustrating cases in which the owners have been successful, and which cases throw into relief another facet of the problem of management of vessels *vis-a-vis* the owners' right to a decree of limitation of liability.

In the case of the *Garden City,* which vessel was in collision with the Polish vessel *Zaglebie Dabrowski* in conditions of visibility restricted by fog resulting in the sinking of the *Garden City* which was totally lost with almost the whole of her cargo, the proceedings for the establishment of liability found the Polish vessel 60 per cent to blame, and her owners then brought an action against the owners of the *Garden City* and all other persons claiming or being entitled to claim damages arising out of the collision, seeking limitation of liability pursuant to the Merchant Shipping Act, 1894, Section 503 (1).

The Court in that case said that the top management of every shipowning corporation ought to institute a system of supervision of navigation and detection of faults, but that here the fact that the organisation regulations of the owners did not provide that supervision of navigation was one of the tasks which was the responsibility of the director of technical and investment affairs, and did not provide that it was one of the tasks of the chief navigator, was not causative of the collision since both the director and the chief navigator were well aware of their responsibilities.

There was a system of inspections in existence by which after every voyage the chief navigator or one of his staff would go on board every vessel of the company when it returned to a Polish port. But it was held, on the evidence, that although the system was, in the opinion of the Court, adequate, it was not perfect. With regard to the owners' instructions as to navigation in restricted visibility, the company did take proper steps to bring to the notice of their masters and deck officers the Regulations for the Prevention of

Collision at Sea and did attain the standard demanded of a reasonable and prudent shipowner in respect of the instructions which they gave to their officers as to navigation in restricted visibility.

The Court held that the owners of the *Zaglebie Dabrowski* were entitled to a decree of limitation of liability and said, amongst other things, that in this case there was no fault on the part of the director or the managing-director in that they did what it was reasonably necessary for the owner of a large number of ships to do, *i.e.,* they appreciated the navigational problems involved by the use of radar in fog and impressed the urgency of such problems upon the masters of their vessels, and took steps to ensure, as far as they reasonably could that their vessels were safely navigated in fog.

An interesting case arose out of the explosion and fire which followed upon the escape of petrol from the *Athelvictor* whilst she was discharging her cargo of petrol in Lagos Harbour. Other ships were sunk or damaged and there was considerable damage to property ashore. There was also loss of life and personal injury sustained ashore and afloat. The owners of the vessel admitted that petroleum spirit escaped from the vessel because certain sea valves were open, and admitted that the loss and damage caused by the fire and explosion was caused by the negligence of those on board the vessel, but sought a decree of limitation of liability.

The claimants disputed that the owners of the vessel were entitled to a decree of limitation, contending that the damage was due, not to negligent management of the ship but to negligence in the management of the cargo. They further contended that if it was caused by negligent management of the ship, no statutory authority entitled the owners to limit their liability in respect of loss of life. The Merchant Shipping Act provides that the owners of a ship will be entitled to limit liability ". . . where all of any of the following occurrences take place, without their actual fault or privity . . ." and among those occurrences is that provided for in Section 503 (1) (c) "where any loss of life or personal injury is caused to any person carried in any other vessel by reason of the improper navigation of the ship". The Court ruled that the negligent failure of the ship's personnel to close the sea valves did not amount to improper navigation of the ship and that therefore the shipowners were not entitled to limit their liability in respect of the life claims or personal injury claims.

In considering the meaning to be given to the words "improper management" of the ship, in a limitation action, the Court was entitled to disregard the narrower construction put on similar words in bill of lading cases, and giving the words their ordinary and natural meaning, "improper management" of the ship included improper management of the ship's appliances where, as in this case, they were fitted for ship and cargo purposes, and covered the negligence of the ship's personnel. It was therefore held that the shipowners were entitled to limit their liability in respect of the damage done to other vessels and property ashore.

We turn now to the extension of Section 503 of the Merchant Shipping Act, 1894, by Section 1 of the Merchant Shipping (Liability of Shipowners and Others) Act, 1900, to damage to property ashore caused by the improper management of the ship without the actual fault or privity of the owner. The case of the *Anonity* is very illustrative of the duties of the owners of vessels, and the nature of the burden of proof upon them to show that such loss or damage was caused without their actual fault or privity, in seeking a decree of limitation of liability.

The *Anonity* was a small tanker which had secured alongside a jetty belonging to London and Thames Haven Oil Wharves and, due to the negligence of those on the tanker in leaving the galley stove burning or smouldering at a time when it should have been turned off completely and thereby allowing sparks to escape from the galley stack on to the jetty, the jetty was destroyed by the fire so caused, and much other property ashore was also damaged.

The owners of the *Anonity* sought to limit their liability on the ground that the occurrence took place without their actual fault or privity. In the trial Court the Judge found that the incident was caused by the improper management of the vessel within the meaning of Section 1 of the Act of 1900, and the burden of proving that the loss and damage was caused without the actual fault or privity of the owners of the vessel now rested with them. In considering whether there had been fault or privity on the part of the owners in the management of their vessel, the owners being a limited company, the Court had to consider the conduct of the person who, by reason of his position, could be said to be the alter ego of the company. The vessel was owned by F.T. Everard & Sons, Ltd., and the person so concerned was Mr. W. Everard who was chairman of the company.

In contesting the action brought by the owners of the vessel to limit their liability, those who had claims against the vessel for the damage caused by the fire alleged that the owners had failed to give clear or adequate instructions about the use of galley stoves on their ships, including the *Anonity,* when such ships were at petroleum installations. In the trial Court it was held that causing or allowing sparks to escape from the stove, which should not have been burning whilst the vessel was alongside the jetty, was improper management of an appliance fitted solely for the ship's purposes, and was, therefore, within Section 1 of the Act of 1900, and that the fire and damage did not occur without the shipowners' actual fault or privity, in that they failed to give adequate and proper notice prohibiting the use of galley fires at oil berths, and that, therefore, the plea for limitation of liability must fail.

It seems that Mr. Everard had given clear instructions about the use of galley fires but the Court found that those instructions were not enough. A letter had been sent to the vessel by the marine superintendent in which instructions were given that galley fires were to be extinguished before berthing at any oil jetty in the U.K. or on the Continent, and they were received by the master of the vessel. But the only action he took was to show the letter to his chief and second officer and then filed the letter in a somewhat haphazard manner and seemingly never looked at it again or took any positive action regarding it.

The case was finally determined in the Court of Appeal when the ruling of the trial Court was upheld that the fire, and damage caused by the fire, did not occur without the actual fault or privity of the shipowners in that they failed to give adequate and proper notice prohibiting the use of galley fires at oil berths and that therefore the shipowners were not entitled to a decree of limitation of liability.

The Court commented that the risk of a galley fire setting alight an oil jetty was the sort of risk that is more appreciated in the prescient contemplation of the boardroom than in the galley of a little ship, and that no doubt to the seaman in the galley, safety restrictions seem to be fussy and unnecessarily pedantry, but in the boardroom it is seen that a disastrous fire might possibly be so caused and that any reasonable precaution that can exclude that possibility must be taken.

That in the view of the Court was what Mr. Everard, the alter ego of the company, should have foreseen and enforced as a reasonable shipowner and that was his personal duty. However, the Court also observed that maybe he could have avoided fault if he had delegated the urgent enforcement of it to the marine superintendent, and if it had been through the negligence of the marine superintendent that the urgency had lost its force. But he did not do so and merely got the marine superintendent to send the circular and carry out normal checks.

Something of a somewhat similar nature was decided in the case of the *Dayspring,* a trawler which came into collision with the tanker *Auspicity,* when the owners of the former vessel sought to limit their liability but failed to secure a decree of limitation of liability for the reason, among others, that they were at fault in failing to insist on the keeping of proper logbooks and that something much more reasonable than a notice in the wheelhouse was required.

Reference should also be made to the case of the *Otterdal* which vessel was in collision with the *Tarbert* which caused the *Tarbert* to sink. The owners of the *Otterdal* sought a decree limiting their liability which was contested by the owners of the *Tarbert.*

The question arose as to whether it could be said that the accident happened without the actual fault or privity of the owner of the *Otterdal,* that is to say without his personal responsibility when there had been a correspondence, extending over many months, which showed that the vessel's steering gear was in such a condition that tinkering at it, as had been done, was no good, and that a thorough overhaul was necessary if it was to be of use at all and that if a thorough overhaul could not put the steering mechanism in order a new one ought to be obtained. No intimation was ever given to the owner that either of these things had taken place, and the Court could not see any justification in these circumstances for the owner allowing the vessel to go to sea without something of that kind having been done.

The collision occurred in the River Mersey and was caused by the faulty steering gear and the sole question for the Court was whether this unseaworthy condition of the vessel existed without the actual fault or privity of the owners of the vessel, having regard to the neglect in management in failing to have the faulty steering gear put right. The Court of Appeal held that there was no justification for the owners, after the history of the steering gear, in allowing the ship to sail on the voyage in question without being assured that something thorough had been done to the steering engine, or that a new one had been installed. The fact of the matter was that the owners had taken a chance, as had been taken on other voyages which had turned out alright, but on this voyage it turned out all wrong and the Court declined to grant a decree of limitation of liability.

Whilst the case of the *Thordoc (LLR — 1937 — 58 — 33)* primarily concerned navigation, it must also be considered in relation to management of ship, in that it involved questions of management and compass adjustment. The case is also of importance because the issues in question were eventually decided by the Privy Council. The facts can be very shortly stated. After loading a cargo of flour and cereals for carriage from Port Arthur, Ontario, to Montreal, the vessel stranded with her cargo on the north shore of Lake Superior and became with her cargo practically a total loss.

The owners of the cargo secured a judgment against the owners of the vessel who then brought an action to limit their liability pursuant to Section 503 of the Merchant Shipping Act 1894.

In the limitation action before the local Canadian Court, the Judge in Admiralty granted a decree limiting the liability of the owners under the provisions of Section 503 of the Merchant Shipping Act 1894, against which ruling the owners of the cargo appealed and the case came before the Exchequer Court of Canada when the appeal was dismissed. There then followed an appeal to the Privy Council, the grounds of the appeal being that the vessel had deviated from her chartered voyage by direction of the general manager of the owners of the vessel even though at the time of the stranding the *Thordoc* was again on her chartered voyage. The appeal was additionally predicated upon the ground that the compass was faulty and the helmsman incompetent.

The Privy Council dismissed the appeal and stated that the deviation, if any (and even assuming it was a fault of somebody for whose fault the owners of the vessel were responsible) had nothing to do with the cargo loss and damage, which was due to improper navigation after the deviation was past and therefore not relevant to the petition for limitation of liability. The Court found that there was no actual fault or privity of the owners of the vessel in regard to the condition of the compass which had been adjusted by a compass adjuster of repute before the casualty, and further, that the engagement of the helmsman and his placing at the wheel at the stage of the voyage in question were alike the responsibility and the work of the master of the vessel, and that even if the master was wrong that was not the fault of the owners.

The question of management of a ship, relevant to the Merchant Shipping Acts, came up for consideration in a rather unusual form in the case of the *Thames (LLR — 1940 — 65 — 99. Court of Appeal — 1940 — 67 — 91),* arising out of the hire of a vessel and the position of a hirer in a plea for limitation of liability when issues of management of the vessel arise. The claimant had hired a barge from the owners, and the barge, having been loaded with cargo, sank owing to the chine angle on the bottom having become wasted and cracked which resulted in the barge becoming waterlogged and the cargo thereby damaged. It was found that the damage to the barge was due to wear and tear.

The conditions of the contract for the hire of the vessel were, *inter alia,* that the owners would not be liable for the consequences of any defect, whether patent or latent, in the barge or the gear existing at the time of the hiring or subsequently appearing therein, and that the hirers must therefore satisfy themselves by examination as to seaworthiness and fitness in all respects for which the barge was required and be responsible for all damage or injuries whatsoever done by or received by such barge while on hire. The owner agreed to make good all damage to the barge which was due to wear and tear.

It seems that when the hirer took over the barge he made no enquiries as to when the barge was last inspected, which was in fact a year before the hire commenced, and acknowledged that he always blocked his own barges for inspection every two years. When he sought to limit his liability under the provisions of the Merchant Shipping Acts, the owners of the cargo contested his right to limit liability as he had not the sole charge and management of the barge within the meaning of the Merchant Shipping Act, 1921, and further that the hirer had not shown that the damage occurred without his fault or privity.

The Court found that the hirer had sole charge and management of the barge and that he did not cease to be in sole charge and management of the barge merely because of an arrangement with the owner by which the owner was responsible for keeping the barge in proper repair. Further that there was nothing in the history of the barge to direct the hirer's attention to the defect in the barge, and that therefore he was entitled to limit his liability.

However, that finding was short-lived because the Court of Appeal, in refusing a decree of limitation of liability, found that the hirer, for all practical purposes, had complete and effective control and possession of the barge within the meaning of Section 1 (2) of the Merchant Shipping Act, 1921, which extends the right of limitation to the hirer of any barge who has contracted to take over the sole charge and management thereof and is responsible for the navigation, manning and equipment thereof. The Court said that the mere fact that under the hiring contract the owner had agreed, and had a right to make good, any damage due to wear and tear was insufficient to upset the hirer's claim that he had sole charge and management of the barge.

But the Court found that the hirer, who when he took over the barge had omitted to acquaint himself with the date of the last inspection and therefore was never in a position to know when the next two-yearly inspection was due, had not discharged the onus of proving that the damage occurred without his actual fault or privity, and was not therefore entitled to a decree of limitation of liability.

Reference should also be made here to the case of the *Teal (LLR — 1949 — 82 — 414),* which arose out of the damage caused by an explosion in the barge *Teal* at a wharf in the River Thames. The owners of the barge brought an action to limit their liability, which was contested by the owners of a cargo of whitening in the barge, and by the owners of the café ashore which also sustained damage.

The owners of the barge pleaded that the explosion occurred without their actual fault or privity, and alleged that it was caused by the servants or agents of the owners of the barge. The claimants in the action for compensation disputed that the explosion occurred without the fault or privity of the owners of the barge or that it was caused by the improper navigation or management of the barge by the barge owners' servants or agents.

When the case came before the Court it was held that the owners of the barge had discharged the onus of showing that the explosion and the resultant damage, which was admittedly due to the negligent loading on board the barge of obviously leaky drums containing a dangerous cargo, occurred without their actual fault or privity, in that proper orders had been given to their servants regarding the steps to be taken in handling dangerous cargoes, and that the acceptance by the servants of the owners of the barge of such leaky drums and their stowage on board the barge was improper management of the ship. A decree of limitation of liability was therefore granted.

The reader might also usefully note the remarks of the Judge in that case when he said that he was satisfied that any negligent act of the shipowners' servants which is carried out in furtherance of the cargo-carrying adventure, and which endangers the safety of the ship herself, constitutes improper management of the ship, for the purpose of Section 503 of the Merchant Shipping Act, 1894, even though the negligent act be one which is carried out solely or primarily with reference to the cargo.

In selecting the foregoing cases to succinctly illustrate the interpretation of the Merchant Shipping Acts relative to limitation of liability, the author has endeavoured to provide as wide a coverage as possible and has avoided introducing cases where it is plainly obvious that the owner of a vessel has himself been patently at fault, either in seeing that his vessel is properly managed or has let her go to sea in a patently unseaworthy state either as to her condition or to the condition of her equipment.

● Should the required number of States ratify the Convention on Limitation of Liability for Maritime Claims 1976, bringing into effect some twelve months later the provisions of Schedule 4 of the Merchant Shipping Act, 1979, these present notes will have to be considered in relation to Article 4 of the 1979 Act under which the words "actual fault or privity" are substituted by the words "personal act or omission" amongst other things. (See notes under "Outlook for the future".)

CHAPTER VIII

Master and/or other officers part-owners of colliding vessel

Interpretation of Section 503 of Merchant Shipping Act in regard thereto.

THE words "actual fault or privity" contained in Section 503 of the Merchant Shipping Act, 1894, in relation to the provision that the owners of a ship shall not be liable in certain circumstances beyond an amount specified in the Act, as amended from time to time, based upon the vessel's tonnage, in the event that such loss or damage takes place without the actual fault or privity of the owner, infer something personal to the owner, something blameworthy in him as distinguished from constructive fault or privity such as the fault or privity of his servants.

The burden of proof is upon the owners of a vessel seeking to limit their liability under the provisions of the Act, to show that such loss or damage to property caused by their vessel arose without their actual fault or privity. But because of this important facet in the problem of the right to limit liability under Section 503, it is not enough that the owners of the vessel prove that somebody else, one of their servants, for instance, was to blame for the collision or other circumstances resulting in the damage. They must go very much further and show that such damage was caused without their own personal fault.

It therefore follows that the owners seeking a decree of limitation of liability must examine most carefully whether, despite the fact that they were not on the bridge of the vessel in charge of the navigation of the ship at the time of the casualty, and despite the fact that such navigation was in the sole charge of their servants, there was any fault or omission on their part which might be said to have caused or contributed to the casualty. The special situation in this respect with regard to a limited company is referred to in the chapter captioned "Alter Ego", and the reader is also referred to the chapter on "Provision of charts". But this present chapter is an attempt to throw some light on the peculiar situation that may arise when an owner of a vessel, or a part-owner, does in fact happen to be on board the vessel at the time of the casualty.

In this connection reference is made in the first place to the case of the *Hans Hoth (LLR — 1952 — 2 — 341)* which vessel was involved in a collision with the *Halladale* at the entrance to Dover Harbour. At the time of the collision, the German vessel, the *Hans Hoth,* was owned by three persons, one of whom was the master of the vessel at the time of the casualty. Also on the bridge with the master was a compulsory pilot. Following upon the collision, which was admittedly due to the improper navigation of the *Hans*

Hoth by her pilot who, it was alleged, was solely in charge of her navigation for the purpose of taking the vessel into Dover Harbour, the owners of the vessel admitted liability in respect of the collision but sought to limit their liability in respect of the damage done to the British-owned vessel, the *Halladale.*

The *Hans Hoth* was bound for Dover with a cargo of timber and arrived at the entrance to Dover Harbour in daylight hours and clear visibility. She awaited a pilot and when the pilot came aboard she proceeded to the harbour entrance but the pilot failed to observe the signal exhibited from a mast in the harbour indicating that a vessel was leaving harbour and that no vessel was to approach so as to obstruct the entrance to the harbour whilst the signal was being shown.

Having failed to observe this signal, the *Hans Hoth* pilot proceeded to take the vessel into the harbour under full speed ahead and the *Hans Hoth* struck the *Halladale* with her stem more or less at right-angles. The collision was mainly, if not wholly, due to the *Hans Hoth* entering the harbour against the harbour signals, and for that fault her pilot was admittedly to blame. The question that now arose was whether the master of the *Hans Hoth* should share the responsibility for that fault, in that he was at the time of the collision, and at all material times, on the bridge of the vessel, of which he was part-owner, and was controlling the engines. In addition to the pilot there was a helmsman at the wheel and forward there was an officer and one man preparing to let go the anchor, which they would be required to do after the vessel got into the harbour.

The owners of the *Halladale,* in resisting the claim for limitation of liability put forward by the owners of the *Hans Hoth,* denied that the pilot was in sole charge of the navigation of the vessel at the time of the collision. They further said that if (which was denied) the improper navigation was that of the pilot, such navigation took place in the presence of and was authorised and adopted by the master. They contended amongst other things that the collision occurred with the actual fault and/or privity of the master in that he failed to keep a good look-out or to cause a good look out to be kept; failed to inform himself as to the traffic control signals displayed at Dover Harbour and/or failed to act upon them or to cause the pilot properly to act upon them; improperly caused or allowed the *Hans Hoth* to enter Dover Harbour against the signals displayed at Dover Harbour; and failed to maintain and/or assume command and/or control of the vessel.

The owners of the vessel contended that if the master of the vessel was on the bridge at any material time, he was at no material time responsible for or in charge of the navigation or management of the *Hans Hoth,* nor did he authorise or adopt the pilot's navigation or management of the vessel at the material time or at any previous or subsequent time, and that all orders for the subsequent navigation of the vessel after the pilot came aboard while approaching and entering the harbour were made and/or given by the pilot and were matters peculiarly within the duty, skill and competence of the pilot; and the master, relying upon the skill and local knowledge of the pilot, handed over to the pilot complete control of the navigation of the vessel for the purpose of taking her into Dover Harbour, a port with which the master was unfamiliar. Finally it was submitted that at no material time did the master give any orders or otherwise seek to control or direct the navigation of the *Hans Hoth*.

So far as the two owners, apart from the master, were concerned, it was conceded that they were entitled to a decree of limitation of liability, but it was by no means conceded that that the other owner, namely the master, was so entitled. The question which now had to be decided by the Court was whether the master must share in the responsibility for the fault of the pilot leading to the collision.

Dealing with the contentions of the owners of the two vessels, the Court said, *inter alia,* that it was not blameworthy not to post a look-out forward, having regard to the clear weather obtaining at the time; that although there was a duty of assistance in navigation on the part of the master towards a compulsory pilot, that duty did not extend to matters of purely local significance, which would be within the knowledge of the pilot himself; and that accordingly, in spite of the master's failure to acquaint himself with the significance of local signals, he was entitled to a decree of limitation of liability under the provisions of Section 503.

Another case to which reference might usefully be made here is that of the *Mint (LLR — 59 — 257)* which concerned the collision between a sailing barge and a drifter in the North Sea. Both the master and mate of the drifter *Mint* were part-owners of the vessel and the collision arose out of their actual fault or privity, which was admitted. When the owners of the vessel brought a claim before the Court for a decree of limitation of liability under the provisions of Section 503, the Court held that the owners of the vessel were entitled to limit their liability except insofar as the master and mate were concerned.

Almost by way of contrast, mention must be made too of the case of the *Annie Hay* in which was concerned the question of whether the owner of this vessel who, because of negligent navigation on his part, collided with and sank a motor yacht, was entitled to limit his liability under the provisions of the Merchant Shipping Act, 1894 as amended by the Merchant Shipping (Liability of Shipowners and Others) Act, 1958. The owner of the *Annie Hay,* at the time of the casualty, was acting as master of the vessel and was in sole charge of the navigation.

The vessel was acting as a patrol boat during a power-boat race. The motor yacht *Rosewarne* was returning to the River Fal after a short pleasure cruise. It seems that the owner of the *Annie Hay* was at the helm of the vessel in the wheelhouse with the engine controls close at hand but was unaware of the presence of the *Rosewarne,* and collided with her, causing such damage as to result in the sinking of the *Rosewarne.* It was agreed that the collision was caused, mainly, at any rate, by the negligence of the owner of the *Annie Hay* whilst navigating his vessel.

Relevant to the claim of the owner of the *Annie Hay* for a decree of limitation of liability, which was resisted by those claiming damages from him in consequence of the loss sustained by them arising out of the collision (namely the owner of the *Rosewarne,* the charterers, and sub-charterer and others) were the provisions of Section 3 (2) of the Act of 1958, which provided that "... in relation to a claim arising from the act or omission of any person in his capacity as master or member of the crew or (otherwise than in that capacity) in the course of his employment as a servant of the owners or of any such person as is mentioned in subsection (1) of this section:- (a) the persons whose liability is excluded or limited as aforesaid shall also include the master, member of the crew or servant, and, in case where the master or member of the crew is a servant of a person whose liability would not be excluded or limited apart from this paragraph, the persons whose servant he is; and (b) the liability of the master, member of the crew or servant himself shall be excluded or limited as aforesaid notwithstanding his actual fault or privity in that capacity except in cases mentioned in paragraph (ii) of section five hundred and two of the said Act of 1894."

The owner of the *Annie Hay* alleged that the claims being made against him were in his capacity as master and that in accordance with the natural meaning of the words in Section 3 (2) he was entitled to limit his liability. The claimants contended that the owner was not entitled to so limit his liability and said that in the context of Section 3 (2) the persons referred to were employees, and that in the context of the act the persons entitled to limit liability were employers.

It was held that the words "any person in his capacity as master" were wide enough to include the owner of the *Annie Hay,* and that he was entitled to limit his liability.

CHAPTER IX

Pilotage

Collisions arising out of fault or neglect in pilotage. Some facets of the problem of limitation of liability in relation thereto.

SINCE the words "actual fault or privity" contained in Section 503 of the Merchant Shipping Act, 1894, infer something personal to the owner of the vessel or, in the case of a company, something personal to the boardroom or directorate, something blameworthy, as distinguished from constructive fault or privity such as the faults or privity of the servants or agents of the owner or company owning the vessel, it is somewhat difficult to conceive, on the face of the matter, that such persons should be denied the right of limitation of liability when loss or damage is caused by negligence or fault in matters of pilotage. However, it is not enough that the owners of a vessel pleading for a decree of limitation of liability should prove that someone else, one of their servants, for instance, was to blame for the collision or damage caused by their vessel and they must go further and show that it occurred without their own personal fault.

For the purpose of providing some guidelines on the problems that may arise out of limitation of liability in the case of fault or neglect in the pilotage of a vessel, three particular cases have been selected, namely the case of the *England* which was concerned with a collision in the River Thames and involved the alleged failure of the owners of the vessel to instruct the master not to navigate in the river without a pilot; the case of the *Hans Hoth,* arising out of a collision at the entrance to Dover Harbour involving the duty of the master to the pilot; and the case of the *Quitador (LLR — 31 — 129)* involving a pilot's error of judgment during a trial trip of the vessel

The collision in the case of the *England* occurred in the River Thames during the hours of darkness in the early morning of December 20, 1963. The other vessel involved was the *Alletta* a vessel of some 500 tons which had been loading a cargo at Ford's jetty at Dagenham, Essex. In the ordinary course of events she would have finished loading and would have sailed about 6 a.m. It was contemplated that a Trinity House pilot would take the vessel downriver but, unexpectedly, loading finished before 3 a.m. The master of the vessel was urgently requested to move the *Alletta* from her jetty to make room for another vessel. He agreed and without a pilot he moved the vessel, intending to proceed to an anchorage in the river some two miles from the berth, where he would await a pilot.

The *Alletta* was facing downriver with her port side to the jetty and it seems that the master of the vessel failed to keep a proper look-out which would have showed that there was traffic in the river, including the *England* which would be endangered if he were to embark on or carry out his contemplated manoeuvre. He failed to give the whistle signal required by the Port of London river by-laws before moving away from the jetty, and turned to starboard across the river, intending to cross to the other side and head upstream for the anchorage. In so doing he failed to give the whistle signal required by the by-laws for that turning manoeuvre and, in the event, collided with the *England,* and thereafter there were collisions with other craft. In the action to establish responsibility for the collision, the Court found the *Alletta* four-fifths to blame for, *inter alia,* breaches of the Port of London by-laws.

The claimants in the action for limitation of liability under Section 503 were the successors in title of the owners of the *Alletta.* The owners of the *England* sought to deny the right of limitation of liability on the ground that the collision was caused or contributed to by the actual fault or privity of the managing owner of the *Alletta* in that he failed to take any adequate steps by way of express instructions or otherwise to ensure that the master of the vessel did not navigate in the River Thames without taking on board a pilot or a waterman. Also that he failed to take any adequate steps to ensure that the master had sufficient knowledge himself to navigate in the River Thames and in particular to ensure that there were on board copies of the Port of London River by-laws or any other document setting out the rules of navigation and the sound signals applicable to the river.

There was evidence that the day-to-day running of the vessel was left to the discretion of the master, and that, as a matter of practice, questions of pilotage were left to the master's discretion. When the case came before the trial Court it was held that the practice in this case was reasonable and that the managing owner was not at fault in leaving the decision whether or not to take a pilot, to the master's discretion. The Court also found that the master had been competent and conscientious, and that, therefore, the managing owner was entitled to foresee (i) that the master would not navigate in the River Thames without a pilot unless he felt competent to do so, and that (ii) before doing so the master would have familiarised himself with the Port of London River by-laws. Further that the provision on board vessels of port regulations is something which is essentially within the province of the master, who is responsible for the navigation of the vessel, and well within his competence. The application for a decree of limitation of liability was granted.

There was an appeal against the ruling of the Court that the managing owner of the *Alletta* was entitled to limit liability in respect of the collision, on the ground that the learned Judge was wrong in finding that it had been proved that the collision occurred without the managing owner's fault or privity, and that having found that the managing owner should have foreseen, if he had applied his mind to the question, that the *Alletta* might be navigated in the River Thames without a pilot, the Judge should have held that the managing owner was at fault in failing either to order the master of the vessel never to navigate in the River Thames without a pilot or to provide the master with a copy of the Port of London River By-Laws.

It was further submitted to the Court of Appeal that the Judge was wrong, amongst other things, in finding that the managing owner was entitled to foresee that the master would conduct himself as a competent and conscientious master should, and was not entitled to foresee that the master would not navigate in the River Thames without a pilot unless he felt competent to do so; neither that he was entitled to foresee that before doing so the master would have familiarised himself with the Port of London by-laws nor that he was entitled to foresee in his own interests that the master would have a copy of the by-laws on board the vessel.

The Court of Appeal, in deciding that the decree of limitation should not have been ordered, said that in the circumstances the managing owner ought to have foreseen that without specific instructions, the master, however competent, might fail to have the by-laws available or fail to study them, and that, therefore the managing owner was under a duty at least to give specific instructions to the master that in trading to the Port of London he must have available a copy of the by-laws.

The Court of Appeal also ruled that the evidence did not establish the existence of a practice that owners expected their masters to obtain for themselves copies of the regulations for foreign ports, and that the managing owner had failed to disprove that the absence of the by-laws on board the vessel was a contributory cause of the casualty. The appeal was allowed and the Court ruled that the decree of limitation should not have been ordered. (See also chapter on "Duty of owner to provide charts, documents, by-laws, etc., to vessel.")

The case of the *Hans Hoth* arose out of the collision between this vessel and the steamship *Halladale* near the eastern entrance to Dover Harbour. The owners of the *Hans Hoth* admitted liability for the collision but sought to limit their liability under Section 503. Whilst in this chapter we are presently looking at the effect of the act in connection with pilotage, the case has an additional interest in that the master of the vessel was part-owner.

So far as the casualty was concerned, the *Hans Hoth* was on a voyage from Karlskrona to Dover, laden with a cargo of timber and carrying two passengers, when she collided and caused damage to the *Halladale*. There was no loss of life or personal injury in consequence of the collision, which was admittedly caused by the improper navigation of the *Hans Hoth*. She had arrived off the entrance to Dover Harbour in daylight and clear weather and was exhibiting the appropriate signal requesting a pilot and a pilot was duly despatched to the vessel when she was lying in a position about half-a-mile outside the entrance to the harbour.

From a mast near the southern end of the eastern arm of the breakwater, a signal was being exhibited indicating that a vessel was leaving harbour and that no vessel was to approach so as to obstruct the entrance whilst the signal was being shown. It seems that for some reason or other, the pilot of the *Hans Hoth* failed to observe that this signal was being exhibited, and, notwithstanding the fact that it was being exhibited, he took the vessel in in the usual way ordering the engines full speed ahead. When the *Hans Hoth* was right in the jaws of the entrance to the harbour, more or less abreast of the end of the eastern arm, those in charge of her suddenly saw the *Halladale* approaching on a crossing course broad on their starboard bow and at very close quarters. Both vessels were proceeding at speed and the *Hans Hoth* struck the other vessel more or less at right-angles causing considerable damage. The cause of the casualty was admittedly due to the negligence on the part of the pilot.

In the plea for a decree of limitation of liability, difficulty arose because one of the three owners, in addition to being a part-owner, was also acting as master of the vessel at the time when the collision occurred. It was conceded that two of the individuals were entitled to a decree of limitation of liability but it was argued that the other individual, the master of the vessel, was not so entitled.

There was criticism of the master's conduct in that he was aware that signals were exhibited at Dover for the purpose of controlling the traffic, and that he failed to post a look-out forward. Also that he failed to acquaint himself, from handbooks in his possession, with Dover Harbour signals which would have enabled him to warn the pilot. This raised the issue of what has been termed "divided command" and the risks that might be caused by undue interference by the master of the vessel with the pilot's conduct. But side-by-side with that principle is the other principle that the pilot is entitled to the fullest assistance of a competent master and crew and of a competent look-out.

In all these cases of collisions arising during the period that the pilot is navigating, when a plea arises for a decree of limitation of liability upon the ground that the collision occurred without the actual fault or privity of the owner of the vessel, these facts must be borne in mind. So far as this case is concerned, it offers a great deal of guidance on the problem because when the case came before the Admiralty Division the Court held that in the particular circumstances here, fine and clear weather etc., with a ship of the class of the *Hans Hoth,* a vessel of some 374 tons, it was not blameworthy to fail to post a look-out forward. Also that although there was a duty of assistance in navigation on the part of the master to a compulsory pilot, that duty did not extend to matters of purely local significance which would be within the particular knowledge of the pilot himself. It was therefore held that despite the failure of the master to acquaint himself with the significance of local signals, he was entitled to a limitation decree.

Looking at the question of the duties of the master of a vessel after the pilot has boarded, it is interesting to look at some comments of Mr. Justice Willmer, as he then was, in this particular case. It would, he said, be putting too much on a master, and would be asking him to exercise more than ordinary care, to regard him as being under a duty to know all the local signals when he has a pilot on board the vessel, or to expect him to be ready to query the pilot's actions in relation to such local signals.

In his opinion, on such matters of purely local knowledge, a master exercising ordinary and reasonable care is entitled to rely on the guidance which he obtains from the local pilot. The Judge commented that after all it is for the reason that he has this local knowledge, and for no other reason, that the ship takes a pilot at all. Further that even if the master of a ship visiting a strange port does take the trouble to read up in advance from some official publication what the local signals are at the port he is to visit, it does not follow that when he gets there he will not find that the signals have been changed overnight by some edict of the responsible harbour authority.

To conclude this particular chapter, reference has to be made to the case of the *Quitador (LLR — 1928 — 31 — 129),* which vessel, whilst undergoing trials and carrying out a turning test, collided with a barge and sank her. At the time of the collision, the *Quitador* was in the charge of a pilot and also on the bridge was a representative of the buyers of the vessel engaged in checking the turning movements. The owners of the *Quitador* admitted liability for the collision, but claimed a decree of limitation of liability, which was opposed by the owners of the barge.

The question that arose was whether the collision was caused or contributed to without the actual fault or privity of the owners of the vessel. Allegations were made by the owners of the barge that the steering gear of the vessel was defective with the privity of the owners, of which defect the owners knew or should have known. The Court found that the collision was due to an error in judgment of the pilot and that the collision occurred without the fault or privity of the owners of the vessel. The decree for limitation of liability under Section 503 was therefore granted.

The *Charles Livingston,* meanwhile was a pilot boat belonging to the Mersey Docks and Harbour Board and she was lost due to the admittedly improper navigation of the vessel. She had no certificated master on board, which gave rise to questions as to whether the Harbour Board were entitled to limit their liability in respect of the loss of life claims. A number of questions arose concerning whether a pilot boat was a "home trade passenger ship" and whether the appointment of a pilot as second master was justified, bearing in mind the Harbour Board's knowledge of his career. The *Charles Livingston* was not equipped with grab-lines or grab-battens. There was an apparent lack of line-throwing apparatus and under-manning was alleged, all of which was used by the claimants to defeat the plea of the Harbour Board for a decree of limitation of liability under the provisions of Section 503 of the Merchant Shipping Act, 1894.

When the issue came before the Court for a ruling, it was held that a pilot boat was not a "home-trade passenger ship" requiring the appointment of a duly certificated master, and that alternatively the Board was empowered by the Liverpool Pilotage Order, 1920, to appoint an uncertificated first-class pilot as master. The Court added that it could not be said from the evidence of the career of the second master that he was such a master as a prudent shipowner would not appoint. It was further held that the Board were exempted from equipping the pilot boat with grab-lines etc., and that there was no proof of undermanning, and that the Board were therefore entitled to limit liability. *(LLR — 1941 — 69 — 180.)*

CHAPTER X

Security or bail provided by arrest of vessel

The effect of the Merchant Shipping Act limitation of liability in regard thereto.

THE right of arrest of a vessel as a means of obtaining security in respect of a claim for damages against the owners of that vessel is a subject for examination in its own right, but in the case of a plea for limitation of liability under the provisions of the Merchant Shipping Act, 1894, some very pertinent questions arise as to the amount of the security that may be demanded in order to secure the release of the vessel.

In this connection the reader is referred, so far as the purposes of this book are concerned, to the case of *The Charlotte (LLR — 1921 — 9 — 341)* which vessel was involved in a collision but whose owners sought to have the amount of security to be provided, in order to obtain the release of the vessel, following upon the claim for damages by the owners of the other vessel, to be limited to an amount which would be sufficient to cover their liability under the provisions of the Merchant Shipping Act in the event that their plea for limitation of liability should succeed. The owners of the other vessel demanded that security should be provided to cover the full value of their loss.

The issue became the subject of a legal action when the Court decided that if in an action in respect of damage done by collision, the amount of the claim exceeds the statutory limitation under the provisions of the Merchant Shipping Act, 1894, Section 503, and the owners of the vessel raising the plea of limitation of liability on the ground that the collision occurred without their actual fault or privity are not faced with a denial of their plea by the owners of the other vessel, then the security to be provided in order to release the vessel from arrest need be no more than an amount to cover the statutory limit plus costs. But, on the other hand, if the owners of the vessel claiming damages deny that the loss occurred without the actual fault or privity of the other vessel and deny the right of the owners of that vessel to limit their liability under the provisions of the Act, then security would need to be given to the full value of the loss, that is in the event that the Court should find, in the case of dispute, that the loss did not occur without the actual fault or privity of the owners of the vessel.

The case of the *Coaster (LLR — 1921 — 8 — 368 and 1922 — 10 — 592)* has a particular interest in that it concerned the owners of a colliding vessel being forced to provide security in a foreign port. It was the case of a colliding vessel putting into a French port after collision with a French vessel which sank after the collision together with her cargo. In order to avoid the arrest of their vessel the owners of the *Coaster* had to put up bail which was demanded up to the full value of their vessel at the time. In the subsequent proceedings the *Coaster* was found solely to blame and her owners had to meet the claim of the other vessel under the judgment in the amount of security they had been forced to provide.

Thereafter they brought proceedings in England for limitation of liability under the provisions of Section 503 of the Merchant Shipping Act, 1894, in which action they succeeded. At a subsequent reference a claim was filed by the owners of the cargo in the French vessel and the owners of the *Coaster* also filed a claim for the amount they had paid under the judgment in France, which claim was allowed by the Registrar. There was an appeal when the decision of the Registrar was upheld.

CHAPTER XI

Ships within meaning of the Merchant Shipping Acts

Whether dumb barges in tow were ships within meaning of Act.

LIMITATION of liability is allowed by Section 503 of the Merchant Shipping Act, 1894, in the circumstances set out in Section (1) which provides that:- "The owners of a ship, British or foreign, shall not, where all or any of the following occurrences take place without their actual fault or privity." There then follows a description of the occurrences. A "ship" is defined by Section 742 of the Act as including "every description of a vessel used in navigation not propelled by oars". By Section 508 of the Act it is provided that "nothing in this part of the Act (Part VIII — Liability of Shipowners) shall be construed to lessen or take away any liability to which any master or seaman, being also owner or part-owner of the ship to which he belongs, is subject in his capacity as master or seaman, or to extend to any British ship which is not recognised as a British ship within the meaning of this Act." Also to be considered are the provisions of Section 2 of the Act which provide, *inter alia,* that "Every British ship shall unless exempted from registry be registered under the Act, and a ship required to be registered which is not registered shall not be recognised as a British ship."

With all of this in mind reference is made to the case of the *Harlow,* a tug which, at the time of the events giving rise to the casualty concerned, had five dumb barges in tow, all of which were in the same ownership as the tug. The tug and the tow came into collision with the steamship *Dalton* and caused damage to this vessel. In the accident the tug and one of the barges struck the *Dalton* but another barge made fast to the colliding barge by her weight and momentum contributed to the damage.

The owners of the tug and the barges sought to limit their liability in accordance with the provisions of the Merchant Shipping Act, 1894, to an amount based upon the tonnage of the tug, or alternatively on the tonnage of the tug and the colliding barge. But the owners of the *Dalton* contended that the owners of the tug and the barges could not so limit their liability on the tonnage of any of the barges because the barges were not "ships" or that if they were "ships" they were not registered.

When the dispute came before the Court it was held that the barges, which were not propelled by oars and which were fitted with rudders, were "ships" within the meaning of Sections 503 and 742 of the Merchant Shipping Act, 1894, and that they were entitled to a decree of limitation on the combined tonnage of the tug and the two barges.

Into the consideration of the problem raised in this case there came the combined effect of Section (1) of the Merchant Shipping (Liability of

Shipowners) Act, 1898, and Section 85 Schedule II of the Merchant Shipping Act, 1906, the limitation sections of the Merchant Shipping Act, 1894, which apply to "the owners, builders or other parties interested in any ship" built in the King's Dominions, "from and including the launching of such ship until the registration thereof under Section 2 of the Merchant Shipping Act, 1894."

In this connection the Court said that in view of the provisions of Section 1 of the Act of 1898 and Section 85 Schedule II of the Act of 1906, which admit literal application, the owners of a ship can claim to limit their liability at any time between launching and registration.

Although not directly concerned with the issue as to whether a dumb barge is a ship within the meaning of the act, the case of the *Smjeli* will be found of interest in that this tug and the dumb barge *Transporter III* in tow were both in the same ownership and both held to be ships within the meaning of Part VIII of the Merchant Shipping Act, 1894. The issue concerned in this case arose out of the towing wire parting in a gale and damaging a groyne and causing consequential damage. The council owning the groyne had a cause of action against the tug and the dumb barge and the Court declined to allow the owners of the tug and the barge to limit liability to tonnage of the tug alone, which vessel had a gross registered tonnage of 946, while the barge had a gross registered tonnage of 1,545 tons.

CHAPTER XII

Supervision of navigation

Responsibilities of the shipowner vis-a-vis the provisions of the Merchant Shipping Acts with regard to limitation of liability.

THE primary concern of a shipowner must be safety of life at sea and that, amongst many other things, involves safe navigation which, in turn, demands of the shipowner that the vessel shall be navigated with up-to-date corrected charts and the proper use of radar, to which must be closely linked the proper manning and management of the vessel on the part of the owners, and the maintenance of a seaworthy ship. In order that the reader shall have the opportunity of considering the effects of failures in these respects in relation to the benefit conferred upon the shipowner by the Merchant Shipping Acts, the shipowner's duty has been dealt with in separate chapters. This present chapter is concerned with those considerations to be examined when the vessel has caused damage arising out of matters of negligent navigation, and the question of the burden of the onus of proof upon the shipowner to prove that the accident involving his liability arose without, or was not contributed to by, his actual fault or privity.

It was the case of the *Norman,* which was eventually decided in the House of Lords, which sparked off a new approach to the extent of the duties of shipowners and ship managers, especially in regard to navigational matters, when it was decided that it was no longer permissible for owners or managers to wash their hands completely of all questions of navigation, or to leave everything to the unassisted discretion of their masters. This approach has been followed by the Courts ever since that decision. But firstly, a brief look at the events that led to the *Norman* decision. *(LLR — 1958 — 1 — 141; Ct Appeal — 1959 — 1 — 1; House of Lords — 1960 — 1 — 1.)*

The *Norman* was a trawler which was lost with loss of life when she struck an uncharted rock off Cape Farewell, Greenland. The dependants of the members of the crew who lost their lives brought claims against the owners of the trawler who sought to limit their liability under the provisions of Section 503 of the Merchant Shipping Act, 1894, but the claimants alleged that the vessel was not lost without the actual fault or privity of the owners of the vessel. Their basis for this allegation was that, whilst the *Norman* was at sea, the owners were given new information as to dangers in the area in which the trawler was to be navigated, but this was not passed on to the trawler.

The owners of the *Norman* replied that to wireless new information to the trawler whilst at sea would have been an unnecessary departure from their normal practice, and that they were entitled to rely upon the judgment of their insurers, who would, if they felt necessary, have sent out a general warning to all trawlers fishing in that vicinity. It was submitted that sending out the new information was unnecessary because it related to an area which was already known to the skipper of the trawler to be unsafe, and the area, being in Danish territorial waters, was in an area in which the *Norman,* unless lost, would only be if the skipper was defying the instructions of the owners of the trawler.

It was held by the House of Lords that there was a duty on the owners of the trawler to communicate latest information that would assist navigation, and that the owners' failure to send on the new information was a fault and that the owners had failed to prove that the fault did not contribute to the loss of the vessel and had failed to prove that the loss occurred without their fault or privity. The Court therefore ruled that the owners could not limit their liability.

It is now desirable to leapfrog over a few years to 1984, when there came before the House of Lords that most important case of the *Marion* which has a particular interest here in that, amongst many other matters, it has 'cleared the air' as to the duty of the shipowner to ensure that his vessels are navigated with up-to-date charts. The belief had been held amongst many that whilst the shipowner might not be able to wash his hands of responsibilities as regards the provision of charts and other navigational information, nevertheless, provided he was satisfied that the master of the vessel was fully competent to obtain such charts etc., at the expense of the owners of the vessel, the owners' duty rested there. No longer may the owners of vessels let it rest there.

The *Marion* left Hamburg for Teeside in order to load a cargo there, but because there was no loading berth immediately available for her she came to anchor about a mile from the Tees Fairway buoy. Four days later, when a loading berth became available, she commenced to weigh anchor but she was unable to do so because her anchor had fouled a pipeline on the seabed which carried oil from the Ekofisk Field through Tees Bay to Teeside. As a result of the anchor fouling the pipeline, and the efforts to haul it up, the pipeline was seriously damaged.

There followed an action brought by some 13 companies who were oil companies of one kind or another to recover the loss that they had suffered because of the damage done to the pipeline, alleging that the anchor fouled the pipeline because of the negligence of the servants or agents of the shipowners on board the vessel. The amount of the damages claimed exceeded $25m. The owners of the vessel admitted liability for the fouling of the pipeline and the consequential damage, but began an action of their own against the 13 companies and all other persons having claims in respect of the damage to the pipeline, in which they claimed a decree that they were entitled to have their total liability in respect of the damage done limited to a sum of £982,292.06, pursuant to the relevant provision of the Merchant Shipping Acts.

It was established that the master dropped anchor over the pipeline because he was using an out-of-date and uncorrected chart which did not mark the pipeline. The master had on board a more recent chart which did in fact mark the pipeline but he was not using it. The claimants contested the right of the owners of the vessel to limit their liability, on the ground that the incident had not arisen without the actual fault or privity of the owners of the vessel by reason of their failure to maintain effective supervision of the navigation of the vessel, in that they failed to maintain a proper system for keeping the charts on board the vessel up-to-date whether by replacement or correction. Also by the failure of the managing director of the company appointed to manage the vessel to ensure that a Liberian inspection report regarding the unsatisfactory state of the ship's charts was brought to his attention.

The House of Lords held that it was the duty of the managing director to ensure that an adequate degree of supervision of the navigation of the vessel and of the master of the vessel, so far as the obtaining and keeping of up-to-date charts were concerned, was exercised by himself or by his subordinate managerial staff each of whom was fully qualified to exercise such supervision, and that insofar as the managing director had failed to perform his duty in this respect such failure constituted in law actual fault of the owners of the vessel.

The Court also found a second failing in that when the managing director went to Greece for a period he did not give his subordinate managerial staff instructions, with regard to the matters about which he required to be kept informed, in a sufficiently clear, precise and comprehensive manner. Because the owners of the vessel could not establish that these two faults did not contribute to the damage to the pipeline they could not show that the fouling of the pipeline occurred without their actual fault or privity and therefore they were not entitled to a decree of limitation of liability.

With the underlying responsibilities of the owners of a vessel with regard to the supervision of navigation having been laid down in that case, and in the case of the *Norman,* it is now proposed to turn to other facets of the duties of shipowners in this context. Firstly, the navigation of a vessel in conditions of restricted visibility. Since the owners of a vessel, or their alter ego, are not, except in the odd exceptional case, on the bridge of a ship, it necessarily follows that the navigation is in the hands of the master, but that does not end the matter. There remains, in the hands of the owners, or their alter ego, the duty to supervise, to ensure that their masters are not negligent in the manner in which their ships are navigated.

The introduction of radar into merchant ships created a new problem in relation to navigation in fog and compliance with the rules of the road at sea. Recommendations of the authorities in this connection are matters of extreme importance in the safety of life and property at sea. The transgression of some masters commanding ships fitted with radar in proceeding at excessive speed in fog is a matter which should be within the knowledge and concern of shipowners. Excessive speed in fog is a grave breach of duty and shipowners have the duty to exercise and use all their influence to prevent it. Insofar as high speed in fog is encouraged by radar, the installation of radar requires the particular vigilance of owners and the supervision of their masters to see that there is no negligence in this respect.

For a detailed examination of the duties of a shipowner in this context, reference should be made to the full report of the proceedings in the Court of Appeal in the case of the *Lady Gwendolen*. But the following should acquaint the reader with the basic principles of the duties of the shipowner with regard to the supervision of the navigation of his vessels in fog.

As has been noted, the *Lady Gwendolen,* owned by Arthur Guinness, Son & Co. (Dublin) Ltd., who owned three vessels incidental to their business for distributing their product to Liverpool and Manchester, collided with and sank the motor vessel *Freshfield* whilst she was at anchor in the River Mersey. The collision was due to the complete and inexcusable negligence of the master of the *Lady Gwendolen* in continuing his course in the river at full speed in dense fog, and in failing to have manned, or himself effectively to observe and make use of, the radar installation with which the ship was equipped.

The owners of the *Lady Gwendolen* accepted liability but sought to limit that liability under the Merchant Shipping Act, 1894. But this was contested by those having claims against the vessel arising out of the collision, on the ground that the collision did not occur without the actual fault or privity of the owners in that (1) they failed to instruct the master to place considerations of safety above those of keeping to schedule, or to see that such instructions were observed and failed to instruct the master not to proceed at excessive speed in fog, or to see that the master complied with that instruction, (2) that they failed to ensure that the master and/or mate were properly instructed in the use of radar and failed to instruct the master as to the necessity of the mate being on the bridge when using radar. Evidence was given at the trial that the master habitually proceeded at excessive speed in fog and that at the time of the collision was alone on the bridge with the helmsman with the radar switched on.

The main business of the company was directed by a managing director assisted by three assistant managing directors, one of whom was responsible for traffic, which included the running of the ships. To cut a long story very short, the Court of Appeal found, amongst other things, that insofar as high speed in fog was encouraged by radar, the installation of radar required the particular vigilance of shipowners through the person (in this case the assisting managing director) who was responsible, in the capacity of the owners, for the running of the ships, and that the owners had failed in that vigilance and had failed to consider or appreciate the problems which had arisen through the use of radar and had failed to impress upon their master the gravity of the risks he was taking. It was held that that was a contributory cause of the collision and that therefore the owners had failed to prove that the collision occurred without their actual fault or privity.

Some very forthright comments on the supervision of navigation by shipowners were made by the Court arising out of the collision in the North Sea between the Liberian ship *Garden City* and the Polish ship *Zaglebie Dabrowski* in conditions of fog, resulting in the *Garden City* sinking in deep water with almost the whole of her cargo. In the proceedings to establish liability, the *Zaglebie Dabrowski* was found 60 per cent to blame and the *Garden City* 40 per cent. The owners of the Polish vessel then sought to limit their liability under the provisions of the Merchant Shipping Act, 1894, but it was contested by those having claims against the vessel arising out of the collision, on the ground that there was actual fault or privity on the part of the owners of the vessel in that, amongst other things, they failed to supervise and check how their vessels were navigated especially in fog.

The Court said that the top management of every shipowning corporation should institute a system for the supervision of navigation and that in the case of an individual owning one ship, it may be that he should take on that task himself. As regards individuals or corporations owning many ships, they may properly appoint an employee whom they believe to be competent for the task and entrust it to him. In the case of the owners of the Polish vessel it was a Captain Kuratowski who was entrusted with the task together with the staff of the chief navigator's department. Criticism was made of the organisation regulations, which did not in terms provide that supervision of navigation was one of the tasks within the responsibilities of the director for technical and investment affairs, nor did they in terms provide that it was one of the tasks of the chief navigator. In that respect the organisation regulations were not, the Court said, perfect, but the Court did not find fault in the director general who was responsible for the regulations.

On the evidence it was found that the director of technical and investment affairs was not told, and did not know that the chief navigator and his staff were failing to detect some instances of improper navigation revealed by the vessel's logbook, and the fact that he did not know was due to no personal fault on his part but fault on the part of his subordinates.

In this case the Court found that there was no fault on the part of the director general or the director, in that they did what it was reasonable for the owner of a large number of ships to do, *i.e.,* they appreciated the navigational problems posed by the use of radar in fog, and impressed the urgency of such problems upon the masters of their vessels and took steps to ensure as far as they reasonably could that their vessels were safely navigated in fog. It was held that the owners of the *Zaglebie Dabrowski* were entitled to a decree of limitation.

Another facet of this problem was provided in the limitation action in the case of the *England* which vessel was in collision in the River Thames with the *Alletta.* In the earlier proceedings to establish liability for the collision, the *Alletta* was found four-fifths to blame for, *inter alia,* breaches of the Port of London River by-laws. There followed a claim for limitation of liability brought by the owners of the *Alletta,* but this was contested by the claimants against the vessel arising out of the collision, who contended that the collision was caused or contributed to by actual fault or privity of the managing owner of the *Alletta* in failing to ensure proper supervision of the navigation of the vessel by seeing that the master of the vessel did not navigate in the River Thames without a pilot, and that the master himself had sufficient information to navigate in the River Thames and, in particular, failed to ensure that there were copies of the relevant river by-laws on board the vessel. There was evidence that the day-to-day running of the vessel was left to the discretion of the master, and that, as a matter of practice, questions of pilotage were left to the master's discretion.

In the trial Court it was held that the owners of the *Alletta* were entitled to a decree of limitation of liability, but the Court of Appeal took a different view and decided that in the circumstances, the managing owner ought to have foreseen that, without specific instructions, the master, however competent he might be, might fail to have the Port of London River by-laws available, or study them, and that therefore the managing owner was under a duty at least to give specific instructions to the master that, in trading to the Port of London, he must have available a copy of the by-laws.

It was further held that the evidence did not establish the existence of a practice that owners of vessels expected their masters to obtain for themselves copies of regulations for foreign ports. The Court ruled that the owners of the *Alletta* had failed to disprove that the absence of the by-laws on board the vessel was a contributory cause of the casualty, and that therefore the decree of limitation should not have been ordered.

The supervision of navigation is, of course, very closely linked with matters of management of the vessel, which forms the subject of a separate chapter in this book. Whilst collision of the vessel *Dayspring* with the motor tanker *Auspicity* is largely bound up with the latter, mention of this case should be made here because of its reference to navigational documents. The *Dayspring* was held to be four-fifths to blame for the collision, and her owners sought a decree of limitation of liability under the provisions of the Merchant Shipping Acts.

This was contested by the owners of the *Auspicity,* on the ground that the collision did not occur without the actual fault or privity of the owners of the vessel in that, amongst other things, the owners of the *Dayspring* permitted or caused their vessel to go to sea when it was not possible for the helmsman to see ahead of the vessel over the forecastle, and they failed to ensure that in addition to the helmsman there should always be a look-out on deck in a position where he could see ahead clearly.

Evidence was given that the skipper's standing orders displayed in the wheelhouse, provided *(inter alia)* "Always ensure that there are at least two men in the wheelhouse". Those orders also required that a logbook should be kept, but that rule was not observed. Evidence was also given that in 12 formal investigations, one of which involved the trawler *Winmarleigh* also owned by the same company, Courts had commented on the dangers inherent in the undermanning of bridges on trawlers.

The Court found that the skipper and the mate of the *Dayspring* knew that as a general rule the vessel should not be underway in charge of the helmsman alone but that it was not clear that they regarded that as a rule to be strictly observed, and that comments by the Court of Formal Investigation should have alerted the owners of the *Dayspring* to the importance of having a logbook regularly kept, and that they were at fault in failing to insist on the keeping of proper logbooks, and that something much stronger than the notice in the wheelhouse was required, and that there was a reasonable likelihood that if a proper logbook had been kept, the mate of the vessel would not have left the wheelhouse when he did, leaving the helmsman alone. It was held that there was a causal link between that fault and the casualty, and that therefore the owners of the *Dayspring* had not proved that the collision took place without their fault or privity and were unable to limit their liability.

To sum up, the reader is reminded that in the selection of the law cases relative to the supervision of navigation, the author has only dealt with those cases insofar as they relate to such matters, and other issues that may have been involved in those cases have been discarded.

These cases illustrate that in contested legal actions over the right of the shipowner to limit liability under the provisions of the Merchant Shipping Acts 1894/1979, the owner of the vessel, in his plea for entitlement to a decree of limitation, must not only show that the casualty was caused without his actual fault or privity but also was not contributed to by any actual fault or privity on his part, and that it is not sufficient that he should prove that the casualty was caused through some act or neglect on the part of his agents or servants.

Further it is not sufficient that the owner of the vessel should employ a competent master and leave to him the responsibility to ensure that the vessel is navigated with the aid of up-to-date charts, corrected up-to-date, but he must exercise supervision, not only to ensure that the vessel properly carries up-to-date charts and other navigational aids but to see that the navigation of the vessel is conducted with the aid of up-to-date charts, sailing directions etc. Also that a proper system of supervision of navigation is operated.

Although, as the foregoing will illustrate, the owners of ships cannot divest themselves of certain duties to ensure the safe navigation of their vessels, that is if they are to enjoy the right of limitation of liability under the provisions of the Merchant Shipping Acts, there are, as was illustrated in the case of the *Thordoc* which came before the Privy Council, certain responsibilities which fall squarely into the lap of the master of the vessel. The *Thordoc* stranded on the north shore of Lake Superior and became with her cargo practically a total loss.

The owners of the cargo of cereals and flour obtained judgment in the Canadian Court against the owners of the vessel who then claimed to limit their liability pursuant to Section 503 of the Merchant Shipping Act, 1894. In the limitation action before the local Canadian Court, the Judge in Admiralty granted a decree limiting the liability of the owners under the provisions of Section 503, against which ruling the owners of the cargo appealed and the case came before the Exchequer Court of Canada when the appeal was dismissed. There then followed an appeal to the Privy Council, the grounds of the appeal being that the vessel had deviated from her chartered voyage by direction of the general manager of the owners of the vessel even though at the time of the stranding the *Thordoc* was again on her chartered voyage. Also upon the ground that the compass was faulty and the helmsman incompetent.

The Privy Council dismissed the appeal and stated that the deviation, if any, and even assuming it was a fault of somebody for whose fault the owners of the vessel were responsible, had nothing to do with the cargo loss and damage, which was due to improper navigation after the deviation was past and therefore not relevant to the petition for limitation of liability. The

Court found that there was no actual fault or privity of the owners of the vessel in regard to the condition of the compass which had been adjusted by a compass adjuster of repute before the casualty, and further, that the engagement of the helmsman and the putting of him at the wheel at the stage of the voyage in question were alike the responsibility and the work of the master of the vessel, and that even if the master was wrong that was not the fault of the owners.

These selected cases will provide a study, not only of the nature of the burden of proof upon the shipowner in a limitation action under the provisions of the Merchant Shipping Acts, to show that the casualty, in which a decree of limitation of liability is sought, has not arisen, or has not been contributed to, by his actual fault or privity in the supervision of navigational matters, but also of the manner of the separation of the duties falling upon the owners of the vessel and the master.

CHAPTER XIII

Supply of charts, navigational and operational information

Effect of shipowners' failure to ensure vessel navigated with up-to-date information upon right to limit liability under provisions of Merchant Shipping Acts.

UP-TO-DATE charts, corrected charts and sailing directions and the like are as much a part of the ship's equipment as her compass or her radar and it is the duty of owners of ships to ensure that their vessels are navigated with the aid of such information, which must be available on board the ship, there being a residual responsibility upon the owner or his alter ego to establish a system which will provide a managerial check to detect any failure in these duties. This managerial duty may be delegated to an appropriately qualified subordinate, but there is a responsibility on the owner to ensure that there is a satisfactory degree of managerial supervision in regard to navigation and in particular to ensure the provision of reliable chart portfolios.

Before the case of the *Marion,* which came before the Court of Appeal in April, 1983, there existed among many shipowners the belief that the duty of providing the vessel with up-to-date charts, corrected charts, sailing directions and the like could properly be left to the responsibility of the master of the vessel, that is unless the owner had reason to believe that the master was not carrying out his duties properly in this respect. The case of the *Marion* has now left it beyond doubt that it is not sufficient for the shipowner to so rely on the master of the vessel to obtain the necessary publications and information for navigational purposes.

The Liberian tanker *Marion,* whilst in Hamburg, received orders to proceed to Teesside but after she had crossed the North Sea she did not proceed directly to Tees Bay but steamed slowly on a northerly course whilst the washing of her tanks was completed. She then turned on a southerly course towards Tees Bay but when she was in a position about 2.7 miles east of the Heugh, which is about one mile from the Tees Fairway buoy, she came to anchor. Some four days later she attempted to weigh her anchor but was unable to do so because, as was subsequently discovered, her anchor had fouled an oil pipeline which ran from the Ekofisk Field through Tees Bay to Teesside.

In the result the pipeline was severely damaged and the owners of the pipeline and other companies, mostly oil companies, who had contended that they had suffered loss by reason of the damage to the pipeline, commenced an action against the owners of the ship in which they claimed damages exceeding U.S.$25m. The owners of the *Marion* sought a decree of limitation of liability under the provisions of Section 503 of the Merchant Shipping

Act, 1894, as amended by the Merchant Shipping (Liability of Shipowners and Others) Act, 1958. If the owners were granted a decree of limitation then their liability would amount to £982,292,06.

The owners admitted that the damage was caused partly by the negligence of the master in that the reason that the ship came to anchor so close to the pipeline was that the master was unaware of the existence of the pipeline because he was navigating with an out-of-date chart which had not been corrected up-to-date. The sole issue which was now raised was whether the owners of the ship could be regarded as having established that the incident occurred without their actual fault or privity within the meaning of the Merchant Shipping Acts.

At the time of the incident, the *Marion* was being managed by a company based in London (F.M.S.L.), and it was agreed that where, as in this case, the vessel was owned by one limited company and managed by another limited company, the Court looks to the managing company when considering whether the owners are guilty of actual fault. The Admiralty Court ruled in favour of the granting of a decree of limitation of liability, on the ground that the incident occurred without the actual fault or privity of the owners, but this ruling was reversed on the case coming before the Court of Appeal.

The Court of Appeal said that where there was a particular hazard of accident due to failure to have up-to-date charts on board which was or ought to have been known to the shipowners, then it was their duty to ensure that their vessels were supplied with the latest up-to-date charts and that it was not sufficient that the owner of the vessel should rely on his master to obtain the necessary publications and information for the purpose of navigation.

Also that if top management were under a duty to ensure that their vessels were provided with the latest up-to-date charts then the duty extended to the institution of a proper system, but in this case the managing director of F.M.S.L., the alter ego, was at fault in permitting a situation to exist in which important operational decisions affecting the safety of vessels were undertaken by the operations manager and he was at fault in not providing a proper system of management.

The Court of Appeal ruled that the owners of the *Marion* had failed to discharge their liability to take reasonable steps to ensure the safe navigation of the ship, and that there was a failure on the part of the managing director of F.M.S.L. to ensure that a proper system was established, and that the managing director was guilty of actual fault. It was held that the owners of the *Marion* had not established that the casualty was caused without their actual fault or privity.

Such was the importance and doubt over the issue involved that the case went to the House of Lords where, after a further five days of deliberation, the decision was reached that the loss arising out of the vessel anchoring in the vicinity of the pipeline did not occur without the actual fault of the owners of the vessel. In reaching this conclusion the Court said, *inter alia,* that it was the duty of the managing director to ensure that an adequate degree of supervision of the master of the *Marion,* so far as the obtaining and keeping of up-to-date charts was concerned, was exercised either by himself or by his subordinate managerial staff each of whom was fully qualified to exercise such supervision. Insofar as the managing director failed to perform his duty in this respect, such failure, the Court said, constituted in law actual fault of the owners of the vessel.

There were, therefore, two actual faults of the owners, firstly in the managing director's failure to have a proper system of supervision in relation to charts and, secondly, in failing, when he departed for a period of absence in Greece, to give his subordinate managerial staff instructions with regard to matters about which he required to be kept informed which were sufficiently clear, precise and comprehensive. The Court found that the owners could not establish that these two faults did not contribute to the damage to the pipeline and the ruling of the Court of Appeal was upheld.

As a result of the ruling of the House it would seem that it is no longer good enough in an action for a decree of limitation of liability under the provisions of Section 503 for the shipowner to show that he had appointed a competent master leaving questions of safe navigation, including the obtaining at their expense of all necessary charts and other nautical publications, entirely to him.

The Court said that three requirements with regard to charts had to be fulfilled in order to ensure the safe navigation of the ship. Firstly, the current versions of the relevant charts should be on board and available for use. Secondly, any obsolete or superseded charts should either be destroyed or segregated from current charts in such a way as to avoid any possibility of confusion. Thirdly, the current charts should either be corrected up-to-date at all times or at least such corrections should be made prior to their possible use on any particular voyage.

To recap on the situation existing in the case of the *Marion*, it seems that the system of the managers of the vessel was to make the master of the vessel solely responsible for ensuring that these three requirements were fulfilled, but the Court said that the managing director of the vessel's management company had a duty to ensure that an adequate degree of supervision of the master in the keeping of up-to-date charts was exercised either by himself or by subordinate management staff, and that insofar as the managing director had failed to perform his duty in that respect, such failure constituted actual fault of the shipowners. Since the shipowners had failed to show that the damage to the pipeline had occurred without their actual fault, they were refused a decree of limitation of liability under the provisions of Section 503 of the Merchant Shipping Act, 1894. *(Lloyd's Law Reports — 1984 — Vol. 2 — 1)*.

It is not only in relation to the provision of up-to-date charts, and charts corrected up-to-date, that the owner of a ship must have particular regard, but also in the provision of copies of regulations for foreign ports. The case of the *England* is illustrative of the nature of the duties of the shipowner in this respect, and the consequences, in certain circumstances, of the effect of failure upon the right of limitation of liability under the provisions of the Merchant Shipping Acts.

The case of the *England* arose out of the collision which occurred in the hours of darkness in the early morning of December 20, 1963, when the

Alletta, a vessel of 500 tons, had been loading a cargo at Ford's jetty at Dagenham in the River Thames. In the ordinary course she would have sailed around 6 a.m. when it was contemplated that arrangements would be made for a Trinity House pilot to take the vessel downriver. However, loading finished before 3 a.m., and the master of the vessel was urgently requested to move his vessel from the jetty to make room for another ship.

Without a pilot, the master moved the vessel intending to proceed to an anchorage in the river less than two miles from the berth where he would await a pilot. At that time there was traffic in the river, including the *England,* which would be endangered if he were to embark upon or carry out his intended manoeuvre. In carrying out his manoeuvres the master failed to give the whistle signal required by the Port of London River by-laws before moving away from the jetty, turning to starboard across the river, and in doing so failing to give the whistle signal required by the by-laws for that turning manoeuvre. In the result there was a collision between the *Alletta* and the *England,* other vessels and craft thereafter becoming involved in the collision.

In the action which followed to determine the question of liability, the *Alletta* was found four-fifths to blame for, *inter alia,* breaches of the Port of London River by-laws. There then followed the claim by the successors in title of the owners of the *Alletta,* for a declaration limiting their liability in respect of the damage caused by the collision. When the case came before the Court of Appeal, the Court said that, in the circumstances, the managing owner ought to have foreseen that, without specific instructions, the master of the *Alletta,* however competent, might fail to have the Port of London River by-laws available or fail to study them, and that, therefore, the managing owner was under a duty at least to give specific instructions to the master that, in trading to the port of London, he must have available a copy of the by-laws.

The Court added that the evidence did not establish the existence of a practice that owners expected their masters to obtain for themselves copies of the regulations for foreign ports. It was held that the successors in title of the owners of the *Alletta* had failed to disprove that the absence of the by-laws on board the vessel was a contributory cause of the collision and that, therefore there could be no decree for limitation of liability.

To conclude on this issue, reference must be made to a case frequently referred to in this connection, namely the case of the *Norman,* a trawler which was lost when she struck an uncharted rock off Cape Farewell, Greenland, at night in conditions of fog, resulting in the loss of the trawler and 19 members of her crew.

Whilst the trawler was at sea, her owners were given new information as to dangers in the area in which the vessel was likely to be navigated, but this information was not passed on to the *Norman* as it was felt by the owners of the trawler that to wireless new information to the vessel whilst at sea would have been an unnecessary departure from their normal practice, and that they were entitled to rely on the judgment of their insurers who would if necessary have sent out a general warning to all trawlers fishing in that area. The owners of the trawler further contended that sending out the new information was unnecessary because it related to an area which was already known by the skipper to be unsafe and, being in territorial waters, was an area in which the *Norman,* unless she became lost, would only be if defying the owners' instructions.

This submission was made arising out of the claims against the owners of the trawler by the dependants of those who had lost their lives and the plea on the part of the owners of the vessel for a decree of limitation of liability which was opposed by the claimants. The case eventually reached the House of Lords where it was held, *inter alia,* that there was a duty on the part of the owners of the trawler to communicate latest information that would assist navigation, and that the failure on the part of the owners to do so was a fault. The Court said that the owners of the trawler had failed to prove that that fault did not contribute to the loss of the vessel, and that, therefore, they had failed to prove that the loss occurred without their fault or privity and they could not limit their liability.

The effect of the failure of the owners to communicate information to their masters and ships upon their right to limitation of liability under the provisions of the Merchant Shipping Acts is not limited to navigational matters. In the case of the *Clan Gordon* the owners of the vessel were denied the right to a decree of limitation of their liability arising out of the loss of the vessel with her cargo, because of the failure to transmit to the master of the vessel certain information regarding water ballasting and instructions regarding the retention of water ballast in certain tanks. The vessel capsized and sank together with her cargo when some two days out of New York on a voyage to China.

The vessel sailed with two of her ballast tanks full of water but, when she was two days out, the master, for the purpose of trimming the vessel more by the stern and so giving her more freeboard and additional speed, ordered the water to be pumped out of the tanks. When the tanks were nearly empty, and whilst the course of the ship was being altered, she heeled over, turning turtle and becoming a total loss. The owners of the vessel were held liable to the cargo owners in respect of their loss but they sought a decree of limitation of liability to the cargo owners under the provisions of the Merchant Shipping Act, 1894. But this plea for limitation was denied for the following reasons.

Some years prior to this accident a sister-ship of the *Clan Gordon,* belonging to the same owners, overturned and sank in fine weather in very similar circumstances and consequent upon this loss instructions were prepared by the builders of the vessel for the guidance of masters as to loading this type of ship. These instructions were sent to the owners of the vessel which included a direction that when a ship of this type was loaded with a homogeneous cargo, such as was the case in the loading of the *Clan Gordon,* the water tanks should be full. These instructions were never communicated by the owners of the vessel to the master, possibly because he had had considerable experience of ships of that type.

The Court reached the conclusion that the ship was unseaworthy in certain not improbable conditions unless special precautions were taken which it was the duty of the owners of the vessel to enjoin as being required by the structure of the ship, and having failed to enjoin those instructions the shipowners were liable to the cargo interests in respect of the loss of the cargo. The shipowners' claim for a decree of limitation of liability under the provisions of Section 503 of the Merchant Shipping Act, 1894, was refused because they failed to show that the loss occurred without their actual fault or privity.

On April 14, 1955, a disastrous fire broke out at No. 3 jetty, Thames Haven, when the small tanker *Anonity* was lying at the jetty, resulting in the jetty being destroyed and installations and other property being damaged. The owners of the vessel admitted that the fire was caused by the negligence of those on board the vessel in leaving the galley stove burning or smouldering at a time when it should have been turned off completely, thereby causing or allowing sparks to escape from the galley stack on to the jetty.

The owners of the vessel sought to limit their liability, contending that the negligence constituted improper management of the vessel within the meaning of Section 1 of the Merchant Shipping (Liability of Shipowners and Others) Act, 1900, and claimed that the fire and damage occurred without their fault or privity. They accordingly claimed a decree limiting their liability under the provisions of the Merchant Shipping Acts.

Those claiming from the shipowners in respect of their loss arising out of the damage done by the fire, contended that the cause of the fire did not constitute improper navigation or management of the ship so as to permit the owners to limit their liability, and in the alternative contended that the fire and damages were due to the actual fault or privity of the owners of the vessel, in that they failed to give clear or adequate instructions about the use of the galley stoves on their ships, including the *Anonity* when such ships were at petroleum installations.

It was also claimed that the shipowners had failed to operate disciplinary checks upon the masters of their ships, including the *Anonity,* so as to make them properly responsible for the due observance of statutory prohibitions imposed in the interests of safety. There were also many other allegations of failure on the part of the owners regarding inspection of galley chimneys, inadequate methods of cleaning galley chimneys etc., but the question here is whether adequate instructions were given by the owners of the vessel to their servants as to the extinguishing of galley fires when the *Anonity* was lying alongside the oil jetty.

When the case of the *Anonity* came before Mr. Justice Hewson in the Admiralty Court, it was held that causing or allowing sparks to escape from the stove, which should not have been burning at all while the *Anonity* was alongside the jetty, was improper management of an appliance fitted solely for ship's purposes and was therefore within Section 1 of the Act of 1900, and that the fire and damage did not occur without the shipowners' actual fault or privity in that they failed to give adequate and proper notice prohibiting the use of galley fires at oil berths. The shipowners were therefore refused a decree of limitation of liability. There was an appeal against this ruling but this was dismissed by the Court of Appeal.

The marine superintendent of the shipowners sent out to the masters of the company's vessels a year before the fire two notices, the first being a letter to the safety officer at Purfleet from the deputy terminal manager requesting certain safety precautions. A circular copy of that letter was sent to the masters of all vessels with a covering letter from the marine superintendent requesting that the notice be brought to the immediate attention of officers and crew to ensure that on arrival at the oil jetties galley fires were to be extinguished before berthing.

This, the Court said, was not enough and there ought to have been instructions from the owners that some arresting notice prohibiting the use of galley fires at oil berths should be displayed permanently near the stove, or near the feed-valve to the stove, to warn anyone so minded not to use it, or to light it, at oil jetties.

CHAPTER XIV

Towage contracts

In relation to Section 503 of the Merchant Shipping Act, 1894.

THERE is little legal precedent to establish an overall picture of the effect of the Merchant Shipping Act upon towage contracts when a casualty gives rise to a plea for a decree of limitation of liability under the provisions of Section 503 as subsequently amended. However, the case of the *Kirknes (LLR — 1956 — 2 — 651)* does provide some guidance on the problem. The claim for limitation of liability in this case was made by the owners of the trawler *Kirknes* in respect of the sinking of the tug *Hillman* whilst the latter was towing the *Kirknes.* During the course of the towage, the *Hillman* capsized and sank, four of her crew being drowned.

The owners of the *Hillman* commenced proceedings against the owners of the *Kirknes* claiming damages for negligence, and alternatively a declaration that under the terms of the towage contract entered into between the owners of the *Kirknes* and the owners of the *Hillman,* the owners of the *Kirknes* had accepted liability regardless of negligence to pay for the damage caused by the tug. Claims were also made on behalf of the dependants of the members of the crew of the *Hillman* who had been drowned.

The owners of the *Kirknes* admitted liability but alleged that the casualty was caused by the improper navigation of their vessel and also alleged that the casualty occurred without their actual fault or privity. The question that now arose was whether the owners of the *Kirknes* were precluded by the towage conditions or otherwise from limiting their liability under the provisions of Section 503 of the Merchant Shipping Act, 1894.

The towage contract entered into between the owners of the trawler and the owners of the tug was on terms which incorporated the United Kingdom Standard Towage Conditions, and the most important clause of the conditions for examination here was Clause 3 which provided, *inter alia,* that the "... hirer shall pay for all loss or damage and personal injury or loss of life and shall also indemnify the tug owner against the consequences thereof." The crucial words, for the purpose of the question that now arose, were "the hirer shall pay for all loss or damage and personal injury or loss of life."

What was the effect of these towage conditions on Section 503 of the Act? The Court came to the conclusion that, so far as the tug owners were concerned, the rights of the owners of the *Kirknes* under Section 503 were limited to claims for damages brought in respect of negligent navigation and did not extend to the claim of the tug owners based upon their contractual rights under the towage conditions, and that accordingly the owners of the tug were entitled under their contractual claim to recover in full.

The Court went on to say that, there being no clear provision in the towage conditions which expressly or impliedly excluded the operation of Section 503, that section applied so far as concerned the claim of the owners of the tug for damages in respect of the negligent navigation of the tow.

So far as the life claimants were concerned, the Court said that it was to be inferred that the tugowners in entering into the towage contract were contracting not only on their own behalf but also as agents for their master and crew; but that, the life claimants' claim being for damages for negligence, Section 503 of the Act still applied and the owners of the *Kirknes* were entitled to limit their liability in respect thereof.

One other case has been selected for mention here, namely the *Vigilant (LLR — 1920 — 3 — 55 and 1921 — 7 — 232),* a tug which, in the course of the performance of a contract of towage, improperly transferred her tow rope to another tug in order that she might proceed to the performance of another contract of towage. During the course of the transfer the tow was damaged. The owners of the *Vigilant* sought to limit their liability under Section 503 and alternatively under the combined effect of Section 503 and Section 1 of the Merchant Shipping (Liability of Shipowners and Others) Act, 1900.

The owners of the tow contended that the casualty arose out of a breach of the towage contract, and that a mere breach of a towing contract would not bring the case within the limitation of liability section. When the issue came before the Court it was held that in this case something more than a breach of contract arose, and that the *Vigilant* was engaged in an act of navigation when she transferred the tow rope to another rug. This act, the Court said, was an act of improper navigation within the meaning of Section 503, and therefore the owners of the *Vigilant* were entitled to a decree of limitation of their liability.

CHAPTER XV

Tug and tow

Limitation of liability — when tug and tow in same ownership — when tug and tow in different ownership — basis of limitation vis a vis tonnage of tug and tow — position when grounded vessel taken in tow by sister ship — etc.

A PLEA for a decree of limitation of liability under Section 503 of the Merchant Shipping Act, 1893, when one or more of the vessels concerned are involved in towage in one form or another, gives rise to particular considerations peculiar to damage caused during the performance of such operations. In the case of collision between tug and tow, the vessels involved may be in the same ownership or the one may be under different ownership to the other. In the case of the former, special considerations may apply in determining whether or not there is a right to limitation of liability as compared with the considerations obtaining in the latter case.

A number of cases have been selected which it is felt will provide an understanding of the nature of the problems that may arise and the considerations to be appreciated in the determination of the question as to the right or otherwise to a decree of limitation of liability under the provisions of the Act.

Tug and tow in same ownership

In the case of *The Ran* and *The Graygarth (LLR — 1921 — 8 — 305)*, the latter vessel, a tug, had a number of barges in tow during the course of which the barge *Ran*, which was in the same ownership as the *Graygarth*, collided with and caused damage to another barge, the *Para*. In an action *in rem* by the owners of the barge *Para* against the owners of the barge *Ran* (bail having been given in respect of the *Ran*), the Court found that the collision was solely due to the negligent navigation of those on board the *Graygarth* who had control of the navigation of the *Ran*. It was held that the owners of this barge, as owners of the tug *Graygarth,* were liable.

There then followed an application to the Court for a decree of limitation of liability under Section 503 of the Merchant Shipping Act, 1893, which application was successful to the extent that limitation was granted on the tonnage of the *Graygarth*. That decision was, however, later reversed by the Court of Appeal when it was held that as the action was brought against the barge *Ran* by the owners of the barge *Para* and as the *Ran* was improperly navigated by the servants of the owners of the *Ran,* no matter where those servants were situated, the owners of the barge *Para* were entitled to judgment against the defendants as owners of the *Ran* and the defendants were not entitled to limit their liability on the tonnage of *Graygarth* but must bring their action to limit liability on the basis of the tonnage of the barge *Ran.*

The case of the fishing vessel *Radiant (LLR — 1958 — 2 — 596)* provided a problem of a vastly different nature involving an accident in the course of the towing of a fishing vessel by a sister ship. *The Radiant* grounded at night in the Thames Estuary and was taken in tow by a sister ship, the *Margaret Hamilton.* The tow rope parted and the *Radiant* grounded for a second time. Wire was coiled on the deck of the *Radiant* by the skipper, the end of which was thrown by him to the *Margaret Hamilton* and there made fast. The skipper's legs became caught up in the coil of wire as the *Margaret Hamilton* took up the slack and both his feet were amputated.

There followed a claim by the skipper against the company owning the vessels and against the managing director of the company, alleging that the accident was due to the unseaworthiness of both vessels, owing to their defective equipment, and the negligent navigation of the *Margaret Hamilton,* causing the second grounding. When the case came before the Admiralty Court, it was held that the effective causes of the accident were the grounding of the *Radiant* due to the negligent navigation of the *Margaret Hamilton,* the inadequacy of the ropes, the defective condition of the gear box of the *Margaret Hamilton,* and the absence of a deck light on the *Radiant.* The Court ruled that the skipper was entitled to judgment in full against the company owning the vessels (subject to any limitation of liability). As regards the claim against the managing director (admittedly, in this respect, the "alter ego" of the company) the Court said that he knew (or had the means of knowing) about the defects in the vessels which contributed to the accident, and that there was on his part a failure of management in that no adequate provision was made for periodical inspection.

The Court ruled that accordingly the company had failed to discharge the burden of proof upon them under the provisions of Section 503, of proving that the accident occurred without their actual fault or privity, and that, therefore, the company could not limit their liability under the Act. Further, as regards the managing director, the claimant had discharged the onus of proving that this person was a party to sending the vessels to sea in an unseaworthy condition and that his injury resulted from that condition. It was held that the managing director was liable and that the claimant's right was a personal right against the managing director in his personal capacity and there was no question of his limiting his liability.

Although the Court came to the conclusion in this case that a personal action lay against the managing director on the same facts as actual fault or privity was found against the company, it must not be assumed that this must necessarily be so in all cases. (See the comments of Lord Justice Willmer in the case of the *Anonity*).

The case of the *Harlow (LLR — 10 — 66 — 169 — 244 — 488),* whilst mainly concerned with the question of whether the barges in tow of the tug were ships within the meaning of the Merchant Shipping Act, 1894, also raised an issue of limitation arising out of the tug *Harlow* with five dumb barges in tow, coming into collision with the steamship *Dalton* which was damaged by the collision, the cause of the damage being due to the negligent navigation by the tug owners' servants on the tug and on the barges. The barges were all in the same ownership as the tug.

The tug and one of the barges struck the *Dalton,* but another barge made fast to the colliding barge by her weight and momentum contributed to the damage. The owners of the tug and barges sought to limit their liability to an amount based on the tonnage of the tug, or alternatively on the tonnage of the tug and the colliding barge. The Court ruled that the owners of the tug and barges were entitled to a decree of limitation based on the combined tonnage of the tug and the two barges.

It should be mentioned that there was a second collision, the subject of separate proceedings, when the tug hit another vessel and the owners of the tug claimed that the damage payable to the owners of that vessel should come out of the same limitation fund. It was held that the damage to this other vessel happened upon the same occasion as the damage to the *Dalton* and the damages payable to the vessel damaged in the second collision must come out of one limitation fund.

Another case of a collision between tug and tow and a steamship, when the tug and lighters were under the same ownership, was that of the *Freden (LLR — 1950 — 83 — 427).* The tug and three lighters were proceeding up the River Thames at a time when the steamship *Freden* was moored in the river fore and aft to buoys, heading upriver. The tug had one lighter on the starboard tow rope and one on the port tow rope with another lighter astern of these two lighters. The latter lighter collided with and ran over the after-moorings of the *Freden,* breaking the moorings and causing the *Freden* to part her forward moorings, and at about the same time striking the rudder of the vessel causing serious damage.

The collision was admittedly due to the improper navigation of the tug and the lighter astern and the owners sought to limit their liability to the tonnage of these two vessels. The owners of the *Freden* contended that the collision was not only caused by the improper navigation of the tug and the lighter astern but was caused by the improper navigation of the tug and all three lighters in her tow and that the tonnage of the tug and all three lighters should be taken into account in estimating the limitation fund. The Court found that the owners of the tug and lighters had discharged the onus of proving that the damage caused to the *Freden* was not aggravated by the presence of the two lighters on the port and starboard tow ropes and held that the owners of the tug and lighters were entitled to the limitation decree which they claimed.

The case of the *Sir Joseph Rawlinson (LLR — 1972 — 2 — 437)* established that where a tug and a tow are under common ownership, those owners may limit their liability for collision damage to an amount calculated by reference to the tonnage of the tug alone where there is negligence for which they are liable on the part of the person in charge of the tug but no negligence on the part of anyone on the tow. What happened in this case was that the tug *Danube VIII* and her tow, the dumb barge *Black Deep,* collided at about 05 40 hours one morning with the sludge carrier *Sir Joseph Rawlinson* in the Thames Estuary. The *Sir Joseph Rawlinson* sank with loss of life.

There was a formal investigation when it was found that the collision was caused by the fault of the second officer of the *Sir Joseph Rawlinson* and the master of the tug *Danube VIII*. The demise charterers of both the tug and the dumb barge which she had in tow, applied to the Court for a decree of limitation of liability under the provisions of Section 503. The owners of the *Sir Joseph Rawlinson* agreed that there was no actual fault or privity and that the demise charterers of the tug and her tow were entitled to limit liability; but an issue arose as to whether the demise charterers were entitled to limit their liability to an amount based upon the tonnage of the tug or to an amount based upon the aggregated tonnages of the tug and the tow.

The ruling of the Court was that the only causative negligence was the negligence in the navigation of the tug and not negligence in the navigation of the tow or of both tug and tow, and it was therefore held that the demise charterers were not liable in damages beyond an amount calculated by reference to the tug *Danube VIII*.

The case of the *Smjeli* involved a tug, which, at the time of the events giving rise to this case, had in tow the dumb barge *Transporter III,* in the same ownership as the tug, which was laden with certain platform supporting towers. The tug and the tow were *enroute* from Rotterdam to Yugoslavia. Some seven miles east of Dungeness, the towing hawser parted and the dumb barge, with her sections of platforms for an oil rig, was driven by a southerly gale towards the coast of Kent. She took the ground westward of Folkestone pier causing damage to some groynes which were the property of the District Council of Shepway, and some consequential loss and damage.

Although the owners of the tug and barge (both were in the same ownership) admitted liability they sought to limit their liability under Section 503 to the tonnage of the tug alone, which was 946 gross registered tons, the tonnage of the barge being 1,545 gross registered tons. Whilst the owners of the tug and tow were successful in their plea for a decree of limitation of liability, the Court declined to allow that limitation to be calculated on the tonnage of the tug alone.

The Court said that had the claim against the owners put forward by the Shepway Council depended solely upon the allegation that the master of the tug was negligent in the navigation of the tug, the limit of the owners' liability would have been calculated by reference to the tonnage of the tug alone, but the council also had a cause of action against the barge arising out of the negligent acts or omissions which took place when making arrangements for the towage of the barge when she left Rotterdam. The Court said that a claim for damages would have been successful if a servant of the bargeowner was guilty of those acts or omissions regardless of who owned the tug and that although the owners of the barge were not liable to damages beyond an amount calculated by reference to her tonnage, there was no reason why that liability should be limited to a lesser sum because the owners of the barge also owned the tug.

So the council had a cause of action against the barge and also a cause of action against the tug in that the master was negligent in his navigation of the tug in causing or allowing the wire to part and in failing to seek shelter towards North Foreland and instead attempting to hold the tow in the Dover Strait. The limit of liability was therefore to be calculated on both the tonnage of the tug and the barge in tow. *(LLR — 1982 — 2 — 74).*

Before leaving these selected cases on issues arising when the tug and tow are in the same ownership, it should be mentioned that the case of the *Ran* and the *Graygarth* was decided prior to the amendment to the Merchant Shipping (Liability of Shipowners and Others Act), 1958. Prior to that Act, although it could be said that the owners of a tug were guilty of improper navigation of a barge in the tow, in that they were in control of the movement of the barge through the water, the words "by reason of" in Section 503 (1) (d) of the Merchant Shipping Act, 1894, required the cause of the damage to be regarded also; and, in a case where those on the tug were negligent and those on the tow were not, the cause of the damage was the improper navigation of the tug and not of the tow. The general rule was that tug owners could limit liability by reference to the tug's tonnage, but there was an exception to the rule in cases where tug and tow were in the same ownership. But it may now be questionable whether the case of the *The Ran* may be regarded as good law.

Tug and tow in different ownership

As stated above, there was a general rule in these tug and tow cases that the owners of the tug could limit their liability by reference to the tonnage of the tug. But there was an exception in cases where tug and tow were in the same ownership, seemingly based upon no logical ground whereby the limit was to be found by adding the tonnage of both together. However, Section 503 (1) (d) of the Merchant Shipping Act, 1894, has been amended by the Merchant Shipping (Liability of Shipowners and Others) Act, 1958, so as to read that the "owners of a ship . . . shall not . . . (d) where any loss or damage is caused to property . . . through the act or omission of any person (whether on board the ship or not) in the navigation or management of the ship . . . be liable in damages beyond . . ." The case of the *Bramley Moore (LLR — 1963 — 2 — 429)* established that, by that amendment, tug owners could limit their liability according to the tonnage of the tug alone.

Briefly stated, the casualty, giving rise to the legal action which terminated in the Court of Appeal, arose when the tug *Bramley Moore* was proceeding southbound in the River Mersey with the dumb barge *Buckwheat* made fast to her starboard side and the dumb barge *Millet* in tow astern, when the motor vessel *Egret,* proceeding northbound, came into collision with the *Millet,* which sank, with the result that one of the crew of the *Millet* lost his life and two others were injured. The barges did not belong to the owners of the tug but were being towed under contract.

In the liability proceedings which followed, the Court ruled that the *Egret* and the tug *Bramley Moore* were equally to blame, and gave judgment for the owners of the *Millet* on their claim against the owners of the *Egret* and judgment for the owners of the *Egret* on their counterclaim against the *Bramley Moore* for half the damages sustained by the owners of the *Egret,* including any damages paid by them to the owners of the *Millet* or others.

There then followed the claim of the *Bramley Moore* to limit her liability to a sum based on her tonnage alone. The question arose as to whether the decree of limitation of liability should be based on the combined tonnage of the tug and one or both of the barges, or on the tonnage of the *Bramley Moore* alone. The High Court ruled that the limit of liability under the provisions of Section 503, as amended by the 1958 Act, should be governed by the tonnage of the *Bramley Moore* alone.

There was an appeal by the owners of the *Egret* who argued that the owners of the tug could not limit their liability at all, or, alternatively could limit their liability to the combined tonnage of the whole flotilla or, in the further alternative, could limit their liability to the combined tonnage of the tug and the barge *Millet*. The Appeal Court ruled that under, Section 503, as amended by the 1958 Act, the tug owners could limit their liability according to the tonnage of the tug alone and that the flotilla could not be taken as a unit.

It is of interest that Lord Denning, in this case, commented that the principle underlying the limitation of liability was that the wrongdoer should be liable according to the potentiality of the damage. So that a small tug towing a great liner can do immense damage and should therefore have a high measure of liability. Lord Denning did not think that that was the right approach and that the principle underlying limitation of liability was that the wrongdoer should be liable according to the value of his ship and no more.

CHAPTER XVI

Unseaworthiness

The conception of unseaworthiness within the meaning of the Merchant Shipping Act and some illustrations of contested limitation of liability proceedings in which the issue has been raised in relation thereto.

THE term "unseaworthiness" is one of relativity and the question of the seaworthiness of a vessel has to be considered in connection with the particular connotation in the circumstances of a case in which it is raised. At common law there is a warranty of absolute seaworthiness of a vessel so that contractually a shipowner cannot excuse himself from liability for loss or damage caused by unseaworthiness, even though he may be able to prove that the defect or defects in his vessel could not have been discovered or remedied by any amount of skill or care on the part of the shipowner, his agents or servants. But in the case of the carriage of goods by sea that warranty may be abrogated by a suitable term or terms in the contract of carriage relieving the shipowner from all or any liability for cargo loss or damage caused by the unseaworthiness of the vessel. The Hague Rules and the Hague-Visby Rules, relative to the carriage of goods by sea under contracts evidenced by bills of lading, have reduced this absolute warranty of seaworthiness to one in which the shipowner is required to exercise due diligence to make the vessel seaworthy, before and at the commencement of the voyage.

Seaworthiness is not limited to the condition of the vessel herself to meet with and safely prosecute the voyage through conditions of weather and seas likely to be encountered, but also has in its embrace the proper manning and equipping of the vessel, bunkering, stowage of the cargo stores, water and provisions, charts and other navigational equipment etc. But so far as the Merchant Shipping Act is concerned the question of unseaworthiness is directed in particular to the protection of human life and the regulations in this respect are set out in Sections 457 and 463 of the Act.

Reference here should be made to Section 457 of the Act, Sub-sections (1) and (2). Sub-section (1) provides that:- "If any person sends or attempts to send, or is party to sending or attempting to send, a British ship to sea in such an unseaworthy state that the life of any person is likely to be thereby endangered, he shall in respect of each offence be guilty of a misdemeanour, unless he proves either that he used all reasonable means to insure her being sent to sea in a seaworthy state, or that her going to sea in such an unseaworthy state was, under the circumstances, reasonable and justifiable, and for the purpose of giving that proof he may give evidence in the same manner as any other witness."

Sub-section (2) provides that:- "If the master of a British ship knowingly takes the same to sea in such an unseaworthy state that the life of any person is likely to be thereby endangered, he shall in respect of each offence be guilty of a misdmeanour, unless he proves that her going to sea in such an unseaworthy state was, under the circumstances, reasonable and justifiable, and for the purpose of giving such proof he may give evidence in the same manner as any other witness."

There are few reported law cases over the past five or six decades in which the above section of the act has been called into question but it is felt that the reader's attention should be drawn to it. Unseaworthiness is discussed here in relation to, and with particular emphasis upon, the need for the shipowner, or other parties, seeking a decree of limitation of liability, to prove that the loss or damage concerning which a decree is sought, occurred without the actual fault or privity of the shipowner even though the casualty arose out of the unseaworthiness of the vessel.

One of the best illustrations of the position of the shipowner in this respect is to be found in the ill fated voyage of the *Edward Dawson* which vessel, whilst on a voyage from Novorossisk in the Black Sea to Rotterdam with a cargo of benzine, stranded in the mouth of the Scheldt with disastrous consequences resulting in the loss of the vessel and her cargo. The owners of the cargo brought an action against the owners of the vessel for damages for loss of the cargo, alleging that the vessel was unseaworthy at Novorossisk by reason of the defective condition of her boilers and that owing to this unseaworthiness the ship with her cargo was driven ashore and was lost together with her cargo.

Before the ship reached the English Channel, the two centre furnaces were completely salted up so that they had become useless, and two tubes in her boilers had burst. Shortly after passing Dover a strong north-westerly gale with heavy seas was encountered and the master brought her head to the wind as he considered it dangerous to approach the Dutch coast. The boilers were leaking and salt water leaked into the central furnaces which became silted up with salt, so that their capacity was diminished. In the result insufficient power was available to prevent her being driven ashore and she took the ground. As a result of her bumping, the benzine got loose from the tanks and began to get into the furnaces, the result being a conflagration.

The shipowners were a limited company and the managing owners were another limited company (the effect of this is discussed in Chapter II of this book "Alter Ego"). The managing director of that company was the registered managing owner, and the Court found that he knew, or had the means of knowing, of the defective condition of the boilers but gave no special instructions to the captain or chief engineer regarding their supervision and took no steps to prevent the ship putting to sea with her boilers in an unseaworthy condition. The case came eventually before the House of Lords where it was held that the owners of the vessel had failed to discharge the onus which lay upon them of proving that the loss happened without their actual fault or privity.

The limitation action arising out of the collision between the steamship *Otterdal* and the steamship *Tarbert* is another example of an apparent failure on the part of the owners of a ship to ensure that she did not proceed to sea in an unseaworthy state. The *Otterdal* came into collision with the *Tarbert* because of her faulty steering gear, and the fault which was afterwards discovered was a fault which existed at the time the vessel sailed. She therefore sailed in an unseaworthy condition because of the defective state of her steering gear and the question that arose out of the plea of the owners of the *Otterdal* for a decree of limitation of liability was whether that unseaworthiness, that defective condition, existed without the actual fault or privity of the owners. To be successful in obtaining a decree of limitation of liability the owners of the vessel had to prove that the damage caused by the collision was occasioned by a state of things for which the owners had no personal responsibility.

There was a constant history in the correspondence between the master of the vessel and the owners over a period of many months before the accident, of the steering gear being faulty and refusing to act from time to time, but nothing of any importance had been done to remedy the defect. There had been local repairs but the steering engine had never been thoroughly overhauled, and had never been opened up, and it seems apparent that, *had* it been, the defect (which was in one of the valves) would have been discovered. Also it seems that there had been a warning to the master to incur as little expenditure as possible. The shipowners' explanation was that they left everything regarding repairs to the master and his skilled advisers, and that if they did not do what was right the owners of the vessel were not to blame.

The limitation action reached the Court of Appeal where it was found that there was no justification for the owners, after the history of the steering gear, in allowing the vessel to sail on this voyage without being assured that something thorough had been done to the steering engine or a new one had been obtained. The Court said that the owners of the vessel had taken a chance, a chance which had been taken on other voyages when it had turned out alright, but in this case it turned out all wrong. It was held therefore that the owners of the vessel were not entitled to a decree of limitation of liability in respect of the damage done to the other vessel by the collision.

Another case in which the question of seaworthiness arose, and a decree of limitation of liability was refused by the Court of Appeal, was that of the *Bristol City (LLR — 1921 — 8 — 294),* which vessel, whilst being towed from Cardiff, where her engines had been fitted, to Bristol, where the building of the vessel was to be completed, negligently collided with another vessel which was at anchor. The issue of unseaworthiness arose because, at the time of the collision, the *Bristol City* had no windlass, hawse pipes or chain cables, and was fitted with only one anchor and a wire hawser in place of chain cable.

The owners of the *Bristol City* sought to limit their liability for the damage caused to the other vessel by the collision, under the provisions of Section 503 of the Merchant Shipping Act, but when the action seeking a decree of limitation of liability came before the Court of Appeal it was held by the Court that the *Bristol City* was not seaworthy for the contemplated voyage, being insufficiently fitted with ground tackle, which prevented her from anchoring safely which caused the damage to the other vessel, and that the collision occurred by reason of the fact that she was sent to sea in that condition. It was further held that as the shipowners were also shipbuilders they must be taken to have had knowledge of what constituted seaworthiness, and that they had not discharged the onus upon them of establishing that the collision happened without their actual fault or privity and that they were not, therefore, entitled to a limitation decree.

To turn now to illustrations where despite the unseaworthiness of the vessel a decree of limitation of liability was granted, reference in the first place is made to the case of the *Crosby Hall (LLR — 1923 — 14 — 497)* which arose out of the application of the owners of the vessel to limit liability in respect of the damage sustained by the owners of a cargo of sugar which was damaged by reason of water entering a hold of the vessel through a defective valve in the discharge pipe of the captain's bathroom. The Court found that the defect which caused the unseaworthiness was not a latent defect but a defect which had resulted from want of due diligence on the part of the ship's manager, and the owners were liable in damages in respect of the damage caused to the cargo, but it was held that the owners of the vessel were entitled to limit their liability in accordance with the provisions of Section 503.

Reference is made in conclusion to a case in which the defective condition of the vessel's engines resulted in the lock gates of Barton Lock in the Manchester Ship Canal being carried away. The vessel concerned was the *Kathleen (LLR — 22 — 80)* which entered the lock at excessive speed, and when the engineer received the order to put his engines full astern he was unable to get any movement from the engines owing to jamming. There had been two previous accidents of a similar nature, and when the owners brought an action seeking to limit their liability for the damage caused by their vessel to the lock gates, this was contested by the Manchester Ship Canal Company, on the ground that if the owners had taken proper notice of the two previous accidents and had had a proper overhaul of the ship's engines to ensure her seaworthiness, this last accident would not have occurred.

However, the Court held that if the defective condition of the engines was a contributory cause of the accident, that condition existed without the actual fault or privity of the owners of the vessel.

The prime concern of the owner or owners of a ship in relation to seaworthiness is, or should be, the safety of life at sea, and with this in mind one can perhaps vaguely detect from the contested actions before the Courts, when the shipowner has sought a decree of limitation of liability, an inclination of the Courts to have in mind whether the unseaworthiness of the vessel which brought about the damage to other property, was of such a nature as to affect the safe navigation of the ship, or her ability to meet up ·with and safely proceed through the conditions of weather or other hazards, or whether the unseaworthiness was of such a nature as only to endanger the property carried in the ship, for example the damage to a cargo of sugar in the case of the *Crosby Hall.*

But there is one consideration that must always be borne in mind, namely that it is not enough that the fault or neglect giving rise to the unseaworthiness of the ship should be that of a servant or agent of the shipowner, to enable the shipowner to obtain a decree of limitation of liability; the fault or neglect must also be one which is not the fault of the shipowner, or a fault to which the owner is privy either directly or through his alter ego. The question that must also arise is whether the owner or his alter ego had knowledge of the unseaworthy condition of the vessel or had the means of acquiring such knowledge. If the answer to that question is in the affirmative then doubt must fall upon the success of any action brought to secure a decree of limitation of liability under the provisions of Section 503 of the Merchant Shipping Act as amended from time to time.

The case of the *Hildina* is another case of the foundering of a trawler with loss of life, but the issues involved here were not of a navigational kind but involved allegations of unseaworthiness, defective design of the trawl winch and lack of proper instruction as to the operation of the winch. The trawler *Hildina,* whilst on a fishing voyage, and in the course of freeing her trawl which had become fast on the seabed, shipped heavy seas, was overwhelmed and sank. Five of her crew were drowned and another died shortly after rescue. The owners of the trawler sought to limit their liability under the provisions of Section 503 of the Merchant Shipping Act, 1894, but this was opposed by the personal representatives of three of the dead seamen.

In opposing the application to the Court by the owners of the *Hildina* for a decree of limitation of liability, the representatives of the deceased submitted that the sinking of the trawler occurred with the actual fault or privity of the owners in that they caused or allowed the *Hildina* to proceed to sea on a fishing voyage when she was unseaworthy, because the electric power to the trawl winch was automatically cut off when the vessel listed to starboard, and that when the electric power to the winch was cut off, the magnetic disc brake of the winch was automatically applied at full strength and, by reason of this, the winch would not run back when the hand brakes were off unless the electric power was supplied to it. It was further alleged that no tools or applicances to cut the trawl warps were provided in a suitable position and that the skipper, boatswain, or mate of the *Hildina* were not properly instructed in the use of the winch and/or the magnetic disc brake.

The issue came before the Admiralty Court when it was held that the cut-out was not an unseaworthy form of equipment, and that the failure to fit remote control was not an obvious omission, nor was there any evidence that it was the custom to fit remote control. Further, that sufficient instructions as to the hand release mechanism to the magnetic brake had been given. The Court reached the conclusion that the owners of the trawler had proved that they were not guilty of fault or privity of any kind in the provision of proper equipment and were therefore entitled to limit their liability under the provisions of Section 503 of the Merchant Shipping Act, 1894. *(1957 — Lloyd's Law Reports — Vol. 2 — 247.)*

CHAPTER XVII

Wreck raising expenses

Whether expenses constitute loss or damage — whether within coverage of limitation of liability in the Merchant Shipping Acts.

THE Merchant Shipping (Liability of Shipowners and Others) Act, 1900, which amends the Merchant Shipping Act, 1894 with respect to the liability of shipowners and others, provides "(1) The limitation of the liability of the owners of any ship set by Section 503 of the Merchant Shipping Act, 1894 . . . shall extend and apply to all cases where (without their actual fault or privity) any loss or damage is caused to property or rights of any kind, whether on land or water, or whether fixed or movable, by reason of the improper navigation or management of the ship . . . (3) The limitation of liability under this Act shall relate to the whole of any losses and damages which may arise upon any one distinct occasion, although such losses and damages may be sustained by more than one person, and shall apply whether the liability arises at common law or under any General or Private Act of Parliament, and notwithstanding anything contained in such Act."

This Act had the effect of providing a large extension of the relief given to shipowners by the Act of 1894, but that relief extended only so far as to enable shipowners to limit their liability where their liability lay in damages. As will be seen later, in considering the right of a shipowner to include wreck raising expenses in a claim for limitation of liability, emphasis must be placed upon the effect of the words "damage" and "property or rights". The following selected cases will provide a background of various issues that can arise out of the consideration of the problem.

The case of the *Stonedale No. 1 (LLR — 1953 — 2 — 319. Court of Appeal — 1954 — 1 — 291. House of Lords — 1955 — 2 — 9)* is selected in the first place to provide guidance on the question of whether the costs of the raising of a wreck constitute damages within the meaning of the Act of 1900, for the reason that this issue arising out of the sinking, after grounding, of the barge *Stonedale No. 1* in the Manchester Ship Canal, was of such a controversial nature as to lead the case through the Courts to the final ruling in the House of Lords.

This barge was in tow of the tug *Warrendale* in the Manchester Ship Canal, and in the course of the towage grounded in the vicinity of Hooton Wharf and sank, becoming an obstruction in the fairway to the vessels navigating therein. The reason for the sinking was the result of the improper navigation of the tug and the barge by the servants of the owners of the tug but without the actual fault or privity of the owners. The Manchester Ship Canal Company, having at their own expense raised the sunken vessel, then claimed the costs of the raising of the barge. The owners of the barge and the tug sought to have their liability limited in respect of this claim.

The final ruling of the House of Lords was that although the Act of 1900 extended the relief given to shipowners under Section 503 of the Merchant Shipping Act, 1894, it did not enable them to limit liability except where their liability lay in damages, and that the claim made by the Canal Company under the provisions of the Manchester Ship Canal Act, 1936, was a claim to recover as a debt for the expense of raising the sunken vessel and was not a claim for damages under the Act of 1900. The claim for limitation of liability therefore failed.

Turning the clock back a few years, a similar decision was reached in the case of the *Millie (LLR — 1939 — 64 — 318)*, which arose out of the barge *Millie* sinking in the Manchester Ship Canal after a collision for which the *Millie* was admittedly to blame. In an action for limitation of liability the owners of the *Millie* sought to include the expenses incurred by the Manchester Ship Canal Company in raising the *Millie* under their statutory powers.

The Court said that the expenses incurred by the canal company were not "loss or damage" caused to their "property or rights", and that it was doubtful whether it could be said that the expenses were proximately caused by the improper navigation of the *Millie* and that, therefore, the owners of the vessel were not entitled to limitation in respect of the wreck raising expenses.

Although a Court finding in the case of the *Urka (LLR — 1961 — 1 — 363)* on a similar issue resulting in a similar finding, was later referred to by the Court in the case of the *Arabert* as having been wrongly decided, it would not be proper to omit certain details here. In the action in the case of the *Urka,* the owners of this trawler sought to limit their liability in connection with a collision in Stornoway Harbour, as a result of which a coal hulk by the name of *Portugal* was sunk. The owners of the *Urka* accepted that the collision was due to the faulty navigation of their vessel.

The owners of the *Portugal* claimed against the owners of the *Urka* the value of their vessel and, so far as this claim was concerned, it was not disputed that the owners of the *Urka* were entitled to limit their liability under the provisions of the Merchant Shipping Acts. But they also claimed to include in the limitation of liability the costs of the removal of the wreck of the *Portugal.* The Harbour Commissioners had statutory power to require the owners of the wreck to remove it or, in default of compliance, to remove it themselves at the expense of the owners. In this case, the owners of the *Portugal* thought that they could get this done more cheaply than the Harbour Commissioners would be able to do and had the wreck removed by a firm of ship breakers.

It was the costs of this removal that the owners of the *Portugal* now sought to recover from the owners of the *Urka.* The latter, although not disputing their liability for these costs, contended that they were entitled to limit their liability under the provisions of the Merchant Shipping Acts.

The Court ruled that the liability for the expense of removal was not a liability in respect of any "loss or damage" to the owners of the *Portugal* or their "rights", nor was it a liability in respect of any damage to the

Harbour Commissioners' "property or rights". It was simply a liability arising through the exercise by the Harbour Commissioners of their statutory powers, and accordingly the claim did not fall within the terms of the Acts and could not be included in the limitation.

A case of particular interest in this regard (and the case deciding that the ruling in the *Urka* was wrong) was the case of the *Arabert (LLR — 1961 — 1 — 363)*. This vessel and the ship *Cyprian Coast* came into collision, as a result of which the *Cyprian Coast* sank in the port of Newcastle in the vicinity of the No. 7 berth. In the collision liability action, the *Arabert* was held to be wholly to blame for the collision but no question arose of actual fault or privity on the part of the owners of this vessel.

Some five days after the casualty, the Tyne Improvement Commission served the owners of the *Cyprian Coast* with a notice, in exercise of their powers under the Harbours, Docks, and Pier Clauses Act, the Tyne Improvement Acts and Merchant Shipping Acts, that the sunken vessel was, or was likely to become an obstruction or danger to the river and harbour, and to the navigation thereof, and stating their intention to take possession of and to raise, remove or dispose of the vessel, and to sell the vessel so raised and removed. In the event the Commission had the wreck raised by contractors and then handed her over to the owners for removal and drydocking for repair, against the owners' undertaking to repay all costs which the Commission had incurred.

An action was brought by the owners of the *Arabert* for the right to limit their liability under the provisions of the Merchant Shipping Acts to damages payable to the owners of the *Cyprian Coast* in respect of the casualty. There was no dispute as to the liability to pay damages, including therein the item of wreck raising expenses, but an issue arose as to the right of the owners of the *Arabert* to include in the limitation action the wreck raising expenses.

The Court commented that the vital words in Section 503 of the Merchant Shipping Act, 1894, were "be liable in damages", so leading to the principle that "the relief given to the shipowners is in respect of their liability to damages and nothing else". Moreover, although the Act of 1900 undoubtedly provided a large extension to the relief given to the shipowners by the Act of 1894, it has been held to be unarguable that the relief extended so far as to enable shipowners to limit their liability except where their liability lay in damages.

It was, in the opinion of the Court, obvious that a decision that limitation is not available in the case of wreck raising expenses recoverable as a debt by a harbour authority against the owners of the obstructing wreck, irrespective of any question of negligence, is in a different category from the case where the wreck raising expenses incurred by the innocent victim of a collision are properly recoverable as damages for negligence against the wrongdoer. Further, it might be said that that the only common factor is that wreck raising expenses are involved in each case.

The Court, in referring to the cases of the *Stonedale No. 1* and the *Millie,* said that manifestly the inability of these cases to limit liability against the Manchester Ship Canal Company had nothing more to do with this case of the *Arabert* than to establish the proposition that it is liability for damages which founds the right to limitation, and that alone.

In this case of the *Arabert (No. 2),* the Court found that it had been established that there was "damage to" the *Cyprian Coast* caused by the improper navigation of the *Arabert* within the meaning of Section 503, and that the *Arabert* was liable to pay damages to the owners of the *Cyprian Coast* for loss or damage to the vessel. The wreck raising expenses were admittedly recoverable by the *Cyprian Coast* as part of those damages. The Court said that the liability of the *Arabert* for those damages arose *in tort* in that she negligently caused the *Cyprian Coast* to sink, thereby causing damage to the "property" of the owners of the vessel and to their "rights" to her services as a ship. That, the Court said, was the nature of the claim of the owners of the *Cyprian Coast,* and it was the nature of the claim which mattered, that claim being within the meaning of Section 1 of the Merchant Shipping (Liability of Shipowners and Others) Act, 1900. It was therefore held that the *Arabert* was entitled to include wreck raising expenses in her claim for limitation of liability.

So it was that the Court came to a conclusion opposite to that expressed by the Court in the case of the *Urka,* and decided that the ruling of the Court in this latter case was wrong. The question now to be borne in mind, in assessing whether or not a shipowner has the right to include wreck raising expenses in a claim for limitation of liability under the provisions of the Merchant Shipping Acts, is what is the nature of the claim, bearing in mind also that the expenses of raising the *Cyprian Coast,* preparatory to repairing her, were admittedly recoverable against the owners of the *Arabert* as part of the claim for "damages"?

● Should the required number of States ratify the Convention on Limitation of liability for Maritime Claims 1976, schedule 4 of the Merchant Shipping Act 1979 will be brought into effect some twelve months later, one of the provisions of which covers claims in respect of wreck removal etc. (See notes under "Outlook for the future".)

CHAPTER XVIII

Other matters of special interest

1 — Limitation of time for bringing claims against the limitation fund
2 — Limitation when only one claim arises
3 — Meaning of person being carried in ship
4 — Position as regards limitation when cargo owned by crown
5 — Salvage services
6 — When barges operate without motive power

Limitation of time for bringing claims against the limitation fund — Maritime Conventions Act, 1911

WHILST the steamship *Disperser* was towing a lighter on October 31, 1916, a collision occurred between the lighter under tow and another steamship. On the question of liability being brought before the Court it was decided that the *Disperser* was alone to blame for the collision, the judgment being given under date of the 27th March, 1918. On the 8th April, the solicitors acting for the owners of the *Disperser* wrote to the solicitors acting on behalf of the other vessel in connection with the claim for damages against the *Disperser,* in which they said, amongst other things that they had been instructed by the charterers of the lighter to act for them and that the claim was in the neighbourhood of £1,000 and that the total of the two claims would exceed the limit of the liability of the owners of the *Disperser,* and that in the circumstances it would be necessary for them to commence an action for a decree of limitation.

The solicitors for the owners of the other vessel replied to this communication on April 11, stating, amongst other things, that, in any limitation they commenced, their clients would "oppose the claim you intimate that the charterers of the lighter had against the *Disperser*". On May 6 of the following year the owners of the *Disperser* commenced limitation proceedings and on July 14 secured a decree of limitation of liability by which all claims were to be brought in by October 14.

The claim in respect of the lighter was filed on October 7, but the owners of the other vessel opposed it on the ground, *inter alia,* that it was barred by Section 8 of the Maritime Conventions Act, 1911. The registrar disallowed the lighter's claim on the ground that only those who have commenced actions to recover damages or are in a position to maintain an action for damages at the time of the granting of the decree of limitation were entitled to claim against the fund.

On a motion to set aside the Registrar's report, it was held that a decree of limitation of liability under the provisions of Sections 503 and 504 of the

Merchant Shipping Act, 1894, ordering claims to be brought within a given time, does not override the provisions of Section 8 of the Maritime Conventions Act, 1911, which limited the time within which an action should be maintainable. It was also held that if the cause for not issuing a writ in respect of the damage sustained has been the fact that limitation proceedings are pending, that would be a sufficient ground for the exercise by the Court of its discretion (under the proviso to Section 8 of the Maritime Conventions Act, 1911) to extend the time within which an action may be maintained. *(LLR — 1920 — 3 — 88).*

Limitation of time within which to file claims against fund.

An interesting situation arose out of the collision between the *Kronprinz Olav* and another Norwegian vessel in February, 1917. Following upon the collision, the other vessel sank with her cargo, and in March of that year the owners of the cargo on board the vessel commenced an action in the Admiralty Court against the owners of the *Kronprinz Olav.* The Court found both vessels to blame and it was held that these cargo claimants should receive half of the amount of their damage from the owners of the *Kronprinz Olav* who thereupon commenced an action to limit their liability. In February, 1920, they were successful in obtaining a decree limiting their liability under the provisions of Section 503 of the Merchant Shipping Act, 1894.

The decree which they obtained provided that all claims be brought in within three months and claims not so brought in were to be excluded from sharing in the limitation fund. Claims were filed by the owners of the cargo on board the lost vessel, but although the owners of that vessel entered an appearance they took no further steps in the limitation proceedings. But in the meantime, in February 1919, the owners had commenced an action in Norway against the owners of the *Kronprinz Olav,* and in June 1920, when the Registrar made his report in the limitation proceedings, the trial in Norway was still pending and by a summons the owners of the *Kronprinz Olav* asked that the report of the Registrar should not be confirmed and that they might have leave to file a claim against the fund in respect of any liability that they might incur out of the Norwegian proceedings. The Court dismissed the summons and declined to postpone the distribution of the fund.

The owners of the *Kronprinz Olav* appealed, when the Court said that the owners of this vessel had no absolute right to stay the distribution of the fund and bring forward a claim when ascertained, and that limitation proceedings did not contemplate claims by the owners of the vessel and the owners could not file a claim against the fund in their own right. The Court said that if an application had been made in proper form the Court would have a discretion to extend time before distributing the fund; but that having regard to the lapse of time and the fact that the limitation proceedings contemplated claims being brought in promptly and with no unreasonable delay, the lower Court had rightly exercised its discretion. *(LLR — 1920 — 5 — 203.)*

Damage to cargo — When only one claim arises — whether
shipowners entitled to a decree limiting liability
notwithstanding only one claim made or apprehended. —
Merchant Shipping Act, 1894, Section 504.

BILLS of lading were issued by the owners of the vessel *Penelope II* in respect of the carriage of cartons of frozen fish from Mar Del Plata to Piraeus. The cargo became damaged during the voyage and a dispute arose between the cargo owners and ,the shipowners as to the liability of the owners of the vessel in respect of the damage to the cargo. The dispute was referred to arbitration when the arbitrators found in favour of the cargo owners and awarded them 20,540,205 Greek drachmas.

The owners of the vessel then brought an action to limit their liability under the provisions of Section 504 of the Merchant Shipping Act, 1894. Cargo interests submitted that there was no jurisdiction to grant a decree of limitation of liability if there was only one person who had a claim against the shipowners. Section 504 of the Act provides that:-

"Where any liability is alleged to have been incurred by the owner of a British or foreign ship in respect of any occurrence in respect of which his liability is limited under section 503 of this Act and several claims are made or apprehended in respect of that liability then the owner may apply ... to the High Court ... and that Court may determine the amount of the Owner's liability and may distribute that amount rateably among the several claimants and may stay any proceedings pending in any other Court in relation to the same matter ..."

The Admiralty Registrar ordered the trial of a preliminary issue, namely, whether the shipowners were entitled to a decree of limitation of liability notwithstanding that there was only one claim made or apprehended as a result of the occurence in respect of which a decree was sought.

The Admiralty Court ruled *inter alia* that where there was only one person who had a claim against the owner the Court had power to grant a decree or declaration as to the rights of the parties limiting the liability of the owner in accordance with the limit set by Section 503 of the Act, and that in such a case, the powers provided by Section 504 were not required because the only claimant was a party in the limitation action, and the owner did not therefore need a decree which would protect him against other claims made or apprehended.

The answer to the preliminary question posed in this action was that the Court had power to grant the relief sought notwithstanding there was only one claim made and apprehended. *(1979 — Lloyd's Law Reports — Vol. 2 — 42.)*

Salvage services — salvors' diver causes damage to salved
vessel — whether negligent act of diver an act "on board" or in
the "management" of salvors' tug — claim by salvors to limit
liability.

THE action in this case raised an interesting issue, amongst other things, as to whether salvors engaged under Lloyd's Standard Form of Salvage

Agreement could limit their liability, under the provisions of Section 503 of the Merchant Shipping Act, 1894, in respect of damage caused by the negligence of one of their divers in the course of a salvage operation. The *Tojo Maru,* a tanker, had just loaded a cargo of crude oil at Mena al Ahmadi when she was involved in collision with another vessel, in consequence of which she suffered extensive damage to her port side in the way of No. 3 fuel tank which became open to the sea.

In the course of the salvage services, a diver, employed by the salvage contractors, whilst working underwater (having descended from the contractors' tug) negligently fired a bolt through plating into a tank on the *Tojo Maru* which tank had not been gas-freed; in the result an explosion occurred which substantially damaged the vessel. Among the various issues that arose was the question of whether the salvage contractors could limit their liability on the ground that the act of the diver was (a) an act of "person on board" tug or (b) act "in the management" of the tug, within the meaning of Section 503 of the Merchant Shipping Act, 1894.

The Admiralty Court ruled that the negligent act of the diver was not an act of a person "on board" the contractors' tug, or an act "in the management of the contractors' tug" and that the contractors could not limit liability and were liable in full for the damage done to the *Tojo Maru.* That ruling was upheld in the Court of Appeal and House of Lords. *(Lloyd's Law Reports —1969 — 1 — 133 — 1969 — 2 — 193 — 1971 — 1 — 341.)*

Meaning of "person being carried in the ship".

AT the time of the event giving rise to a claim by the wife of the chief engineer against the owners of the motor vessel *Marian M,* in respect of the death of the chief engineer when he fell into the dock on returning to the vessel, the *Marian M* was lying at the port of Teignmouth where she had put in for the purpose of discharging coal. The death of the chief engineer was caused by drowning after falling down a gap between ship and quay at night. It was alleged that the gangway was defective in that a stanchion on the gangway was cracked and of an unsuitable type because it was tubular. The owners of the vessel alleged that the chief engineer was contributorily negligent in that he failed to take care or keep his balance owing to the effects of alcohol.

The owners of the vessel put forward a claim to limit their liability, if any, under the provisions of the Merchant Shipping Act, 1894, Section 503, which, so far as is material to this case provides that:-

"1. The owners of a ship, British or foreign, shall not, where all or any of the following occurrences take place without their actual fault or privity; (that is to say,) (a) where any loss of life or personal injury is caused to any person being carried in the ship ... be liable in damages beyond the following amounts ..."

In other words the owners of a ship could limit their liability in accordance with the limits laid down from time to time.

The governing words in this case were "person being carried in the ship".

The Court ruled that the chief engineer was, at the time of this accident, "being carried" within the meaning of the Act, and that the injury which he sustained was incidental to the ship, and that there was just enough evidence to show that the owners were without fault or privity within Section 503 of the Act, so that, if liable, they would be entitled to limit their liability under the provisions of the Act. *(1958 — Lloyd's Law Reports — Vol. 2 — 179; Court of Appeal — LLR — 1959 — 1 — 264.)*

It was held, and upheld in the Court of Appeal, that the condition of the stanchion had nothing to do with the death of the chief engineer and that, therefore, the claim against the owners of the vessel was unsuccessful.

Vessel sinks with cargo belonging to Crown — limitation not applied to cargo owned by Crown.

THIS was the case of a collision between the vessels *Mineral* and *Myrtlegrove* which resulted in the latter vessel sinking and taking her cargo with her, the cargo being the property of the Crown. In the liability proceedings the Court found the *Mineral* partly to blame, and her owners then made application to the Court to limit their liability under the Merchant Shipping Act. A decree of limitation was granted subject to the rights of the Crown being preserved, it being agreed that no limitation could be obtained as against the cargo owned by the Crown. *(LLR — 1919 — 1 — 289.)*

Barges without motive power — injury to lighterman due to collision between barges in dock — practice of permitting barges to drive down dock without motive power.

THE *Landeer* was a dumb barge and the hirers of the barge had contracted with its registered owners to take over sole possession and control of the barge, and they accepted all risks and indemnified the owners of the barge against all claims. In the events giving rise to the action in this case, the *Landeer* struck another barge in the dock causing injuries to the lighterman on this other barge. The hirers of the *Landeer* accepted liability for the collision, which they admitted was due to the improper navigation of the *Landeer,* but they sought to limit their liability to the injured man under the provisions of Section 503 of the Merchant Shipping Act, 1894, on the ground that the collision occurred without their actual fault or privity.

It was submitted on behalf of the injured man that, at the material time, the barge was not being navigated and that the collision was caused or contributed to by the actual fault or privity of the hirers of the barge *Landeer* in that they caused or allowed the barge to drift or blow across the dock, without means of navigation, when they knew or should have known that that would create the likelihood of collision and damage. It was also submitted that they failed to provide the *Landeer* with a tug, or to provide hitchers, sweeps or oars with which the barge could have been kept under control and prevented from colliding with the other barge or striking the injured man.

Further it was alleged that there was failure by the hirers of the barge to exercise sufficient supervision over their lighterman, or over the transit of the barge across the dock, and that they failed to issue or enforce instructions to ensure the safe and proper navigation of the barge. It was therefore claimed that the hirers were not entitled to a decree of limitation of liability.

In deciding that the hirers of the *Landeer* were entitled to limit their liability, the Court said that the practice of permitting barges to drive down the dock without motive power was not one which necessarily created any danger to other dock users, and that such a matter was properly left to the lighterman in charge who was fully qualified to decide the method of navigation, and further, that in this case the *Landeer* was cast adrift by the act of a third party and not by the voluntary act of the lighterman in charge.

The Court ruled that in the light of experience gained or knowledge obtained up to the time of the accident, there was no failure by the hirers to supply their barge with suitable or adequate equipment, and that in any event the real cause of the accident was the failure of the hirers' lighterman to keep a good look out and that accordingly the hirers had discharged the onus of showing that the accident occurred without their fault or privity and they were, therefore, entitled to limit their liability. *(1955 — 2 — Lloyd's Law Report — 554.)*

INDEX

An alphabetical guide to the subject dealt with and a reference to the chapter in the book where the subject is discussed. Accompanied by a brief synopsis of the background to each individual problem concerned and a reference to the law case under the name of the vessel or vessels involved.

Subject and chapter number	Casaulty or problem involved	Law case
Actual fault or privity of owner or the alter ego — **Chapter I**	Anchor fouls oil pipeline due to vessel being navigated with out-of-date charts	*The Marion*
	Due to excessive speed in fog ship collides with and sinks anchored vessel	*The Lady Gwendolen*
	Loss of crewman — allegedly due to defective rope	*The Covent Garden*
	Ship and cargo lost by fire due to unseaworthiness of vessel	*The Edward Dawson*
Alter Ego **Chapter II**	Due to excessive speed in fog vessel collides with and sinks anchored vessel — assistant managing director the alter ego	*The Lady Gwendolen*
	Due to navigation with out-of-date chart, vessel's anchor fouls oil pipeline — managing director of managing company the alter ego	*The Marion*
	Injury due to defective equipment — managing director the alter ego	*The Radiant*
	Oil jetty and other property ashore destroyed by fire due to sparks from galley fire — chairman of shipowning company alter ego	*The Anonity*
	Ship and cargo lost by fire due to unseaworthiness of vessel — managing director of managing company alter ego	*The Edward Dawson*
	Vessel damaged at berth due to failure of operators of wharf to put up warning notices — managing director of wharf operators alter ego	*The Neapolis II*
Collisions between ships (See also pilotage) — **Chapter III**	Collision in Java Sea — alleged failure of owners in manning of vessel — owners found not at fault	*The Empire Jamaica*
	Collision in North Sea in conditions of restricted visibility — one vessel sinks with her cargo. In this case no fault found on part of directors who took steps to ensure the company's vessel was safely navigated	*The Garden City*

	Collision off Isle of Man — owners of vessel found to be at fault in failure to ensure proper log book kept and to issue proper instructions to crew	*The Dayspring*
	Motor vessel and yacht collide in Falmouth harbour — owner of motor vessel acting as master and found at fault	*The Annie Hay*
	Navigation of barge with assistance of a capstan on board another vessel — barge collides with a merchant ship	*The Alde*
	Submarine in collision with merchant ship at night — responsibility of Board of Admiralty who found to be privy to the fault on the part of the submarine in exhibiting improper lights	*The Truculent*
	Vessel in collision in River Mersey due to being navigated whilst steering gear at fault — owners found to be at fault	*The Otterdal*
	Vessel proceeding at speed in River Mersey in conditions of dense fog collides with and sinks anchored ship. Fault found on part of assistant managing director in failure to properly supervise navigational matters	*The Lady Gwendolen*
Damage to property ashore **Chapter IV**	Damage caused to groynes by large dumb barge after breaking away from tow in English Channel	*The Smjeli*
	Damage to lock gates when vessel's engines fail	*The Kathleen*
	Damage to property ashore when vessel runs aground and goes on fire	*The Edward Dawson*
	Oil jetty and other property destroyed or damaged by fire due to vessel's galley stove being allowed to be in use whilst vessel alongside oil jetty	*The Anonity*
	Petrol escapes from tanker due to failure to close sea valves — explosion and fire — other ships and property ashore damaged	*The Athelvictor*
	Vessel rams dock gates due to negligence in vessel going ahead instead of astern	*The Countess*
Distinct and separate occasions **Chapter V**	Barge in tow of tug collides with steamship and then collides with landing stage	*The Ant*
	Tug with barges in tow in collision with steamship in River Thames — tug later collides with another vessel	*The Harlow (No. 2)*
	Tug with tow releases tow which collides with pier head — shortly after tug comes into collision with other vessels	*The Fastnet*
	Vessel secures alongside another vessel at entrance to harbour — damage done to other	*The Lucullite*

	vessel — vessel casts off and collides with another vessel whilst proceeding into harbour	
Dock owners' and wharf owners' rights to limitation of liability Chapter VI	Barge takes ground after being berthed at wharf in River Thames — vessel's bottom set up	*The Humorist*
	Vessel damaged by fire whilst in dry dock	*The Ruapehu*
	Vessel damaged whilst undergoing repairs	*The City of Edinburgh*
	Vessel takes the ground in the River Neath and suffers damage	*The Neapolis II*
Management of ship Chapter VII	Collision in River Thames — failure of owners of vessel in supply of navigational information to master	*The England*
	Collision — negligent navigation — failure of owners to maintain proper log book and issue instructions	*The Dayspring*
	Explosion on dumb barge due to loading of leaking drums of dangerous cargo	*The Teal*
	Failure of owners of colliding vessel to act adequately on the advice of master as to condition of steering gear	*The Otterdal*
	Galley fire kept burning whilst vessel alongside oil jetty — jetty destroyed by fire. Failure of directorship to ensure obedience to rules and regulations regarding vessels alongside oil wharves or jetties	*The Anonity*
	Sea valves of tanker left open when vessel in port — petroleum spirit escapes causing fire and explosions resulting in damage to other vessels and property ashore — owners found guilty of improper management of vessel	*The Athelvictor*
	Ship anchors and fouls oil pipeline — failure of managing company to ensure vessel properly navigated with up-to-date charts	*The Marion*
	Ship and cargo sink after collision but owners of colliding vessel satisfy Court of proper supervision of navigational matters	*The Garden City*
	Ship proceeds at excessive speed in fog in River Mersey and collides with and sinks anchored vessel. Failure of owners to ensure the proper navigation of their vessels	*The Lady Gwendolen*
	Trawler lost after striking uncharted rock — failure of owners to wireless skipper with new information of danger	*The Norman*
	Unfitness of barge under hire — barge sinks with cargo — failure in management of barge on part of hirer	*The Thames*

	Unseaworthiness caused by failure to maintain boilers in proper condition	*The Edward Dawson*
	Vessel overturns — failure of owners to pass on to master special loading and ballasting instructions for type of vessel issued by builders	*The Clan Gordon*
	Vessel strands and virtually becomes a total loss with her cargo — alleged faulty compass and incompetent helmsman — Court held these matters in charge of the master and not owners' liability in management of vessel	*The Thordoc*
Master and/or other officers part owners of colliding vessel Chapter VIII	Collision between ships at entrance to Dover harbour — pilot on board colliding vessel — master part-owner of vessel	*The Hans Hoth*
	Collision between steam drifter and sailing barge — master and mate of drifter part-owners of vessel	*The Mint*
	Motor vessel and yacht collide — owner of motor vessel acting as master	*The Annie Hay*
Pilotage Chapter IX	Collision at entrance to Dover harbour — failure of pilot to observe harbour signal	*The Hans Hoth*
	Collision — master navigating without pilot in River Thames	*The England*
	Collision whilst vessel undergoing trials in charge of a pilot	*The Quitador*
	Loss of pilot boat due to improper navigation — whether pilot boat within the description "home trade passenger ship"	*The Charles Livingstone*
Security or bail by arrest of vessel Chapter X	Bail in an amount equal to full value of vessel demanded to avoid arrest of vessel — Judgment given in France for full amount of bail — subsequent application before English Court for a decree of limitation of liability	*The Coaster*
	Vessel arrested — whether bail could be limited to an amount to cover limitation of liability under Merchant Shipping Act	*The Charlotte*
Ships within meaning of Merchant Shipping Act Chapter XI	Dumb barge held to be a ship within meaning of Part VIII of the Merchant Shipping Act, 1894 as amended in 1921	*The Smjeli*
	Dumb barges held to be ships within meaning of Sections 503 and 742 of Merchant Shipping Act 1894	*The Harlow*
Supervision of Navigation Chapter XII	Collision in Irish sea — owners' failure to ensure safe navigation by keeping of proper log book and proper instruction in other matters	*The Dayspring*

	Collision in North Sea — vessel and cargo lost — owners of colliding vessel found to have proper system to ensure safe navigation	*The Garden City*
	Collision in River Thames — vessel navigating without pilot and without river by-laws — failure on part of owners of vessel to instruct master in certain navigational matters	*The England*
	Due to excessive speed in fog and failure to make proper use of radar, vessel collides with and sinks anchored vessel — failure of owners to ensure safe navigation	*The Lady Gwendolen*
	Stranding — vessel becomes a virtual total loss together with her cargo — improper navigation — certain matters held to be in hands of master and not owners	*The Thordoc*
	Trawler founders on uncharted rock — failure of owners to radio to master new navigational information	*The Norman*
	Vessel anchors over and fouls oil pipe — failure of owners to ensure vessel navigated with up-to-date charts	*The Marion*
Supply of charts, other navigational and operational information Chapter XIII	Duty of owners to ensure master, officers and crew instructed with regard to rules regarding use of galley fires whilst vessels alongside oil wharves or jetties	*The Anonity*
(This chapter has a close relationship with Chapter XII and should be studied in conjunction therewith)	Duty of owners to ensure vessel supplied with up-to-date charts	*The Marion*
	Duty of owners to pass on to masters, builders' instructions with regard to ballasting of a particular type of vessel	*The Clan Gordon*
	Duty of owners to pass on to skipper of trawler new information regarding navigational hazards	*The Norman*
	Duty of owners to see that master of vessel is supplied with river by-laws	*The England*
Towage contracts in relation to Section 503 of the Merchant Shipping Act Chapter XIV	Tug sinks with loss of life due to the negligence of tow — towage contract — whether tug owners contracted on behalf of crew	*The Kirknes*
	Tug transfers tow rope to another tug to enable her to perform another towage contract — tow damaged — whether owners of tug entitled to a decree of limitation of liability	*The Vigilant*

Tug and tow — limitation of liability when tug and tow in different ownership — when grounded vessel taken in tow by sister ship Chapter XV	Collision — tug and tow in same ownership — action against two — on what tonnage limitation to be assessed	*The Ran and the Graygarth*
	Collision in river between tug and tow — tug and tow in different ownership	*The Bramley Moore*
	Dumb barge breaks away from tug in English Channel and causes damage to groynes — tug and tow in same ownership	*The Smjeli*
	Tug and lighters in collision with moored vessel in river — tug and lighters in one ownership	*The Freden*
	Tug and tow in collision with sludge carrier in Thames Estuary — sludge carrier capsizes and sinks — tug and tow in common ownership — negligence of tug but not of tow	*The Sir Joseph Rawlinson*
	Tug and barge strike steamship causing damage — tug and tow in same ownership	*The Harlow*
	Vessel grounds and taken in tow by sister ship — skipper of tow injured — limitation of liability refused	*The Radiant*
Unseaworthiness Chapter XVI	Failure to maintain steering gear in proper condition — vessel in collision in river	*The Otterdal*
	Newly constructed vessel under tow — no windlass, hawse pipes or chain cables — collision with another vessel at anchor	*The Bristol City*
	Trawler sinks after trawling gear becomes fast on sea bed — alleged defective equipment	*The Hildina*
	Vessel lacking power because of defective boilers runs aground in heavy weather — cargo of benzine leaks into furnaces — ship and cargo destroyed by fire	*The Edward Dawson*
	Water enters hold through defective discharge pipe from master's bathroom	*The Crosby Hall*
Wreck raising expenses Chapter XVII	Barge and tow sink in Manchester Ship Canal	*The Stonedale (No. 1)*
	Coal hulk sinks in harbour after collision	*The Urka*
	Steam barge sinks in Manchester Ship Canal following collision	*The Millie*
	Vessel sinks after being in collision in River Tyne	*The Arabert*
Other matters of interest Chapter XVIII	Collision — decree of limitation obtained providing that all claims be brought within three months otherwise to be excluded from limitation fund	*The Kronsprinz Olav*

Collision — limitation of time for bringing claims against limitation fund — Maritime Conventions Act 1911   *The Disperser*

Meaning of "person being carried in ship"   *The Marian M*

Salvage services — salvors' negligence causes damage to vessel being salved   *The Tojo Maru*

When barges operate without motive power   *The Landeer*

When cargo owned by Crown   *The Mineral*

When only one claim arises   *The Penelope II*